WORKING FOR JUSTICE

the employee's guide to the law
second edition

WORKING FOR JUSTICE

the employee's guide to the law
second edition

Dr. Murray Fairclough
LL.M., Barrister, Ph.D

Otter Publications
Chichester, England

The first edition published in 1996 by Otter Publications.
ISBN 1 899053 06 9

This second edition published in 2000 by Otter Publications, 9 Roman Way, Fishbourne, Chichester, West Sussex, PO19 3QN.

DISCLAIMER

British Library Cataloging in Publication Data

A CIP record for this book is available from the British Library.
ISBN 1 899053 13 1

Acknowledgments

My thanks to Claire Birkinshaw for her invaluable assistance in proof reading this book prior to print and her helpful and considered legal guidance.

Text design by Corpus Publishing Limited.
Cover design by Rob Benson.
Printed and bound in Great Britain.
Distributed in the UK by Gardners Books, Eastbourne.

The Otter Publications logo is reproduced from original artwork by David Kitt.

CONTENTS

Modern employment law, in its many guises, touches the working lives of all individuals who work for another person or business. Until relatively recently the overriding principles were founded in law on the subservient basis of a 'master' employing 'servants'. Since the 1970's such age-old principles have been almost entirely overridden. There now exists in their place a considerable volume of protective legislation, designed to provide employees with a 'floor' of employment rights. Many of these legal provisions are complex, often as a result of directives and decisions created in Europe and which continually amass and evolve year on year.

It is the purpose of this book to guide the layman, in clear and simple terms, through the existing maze of employment legislation. Furthermore, to provide the reader with an easy-to-use handbook on the main legal provisions in respect of their rights as an employee as they currently exist (as at April 2000) in the United Kingdom. With this in mind, the pages ahead should afford self-diagnosis and information that, it is hoped, will be a valuable source of reference for the reader.

Murray Fairclough, Surrey

CHAPTER ONE
EMPLOYMENT STATUS

1.1 WHEN IS AN EMPLOYEE NOT AN EMPLOYEE?

The answer, quite simply, is when that individual is self-employed. The distinction between an employee and a self-employed person has great significance legally. The legal rights of each are different. An employee is entitled to a considerable level of statutory and common law protection, much more than if that person was self-employed. Since it is the aim of this book to inform the employed reader as to their employment rights it follows that the distinction is doubly important.

1.2 THE DEFINITION OF AN EMPLOYEE

An employee is employed under a 'contract of service' or a 'contract of employment' and is different from a self-employed or independent contractor who would typically work under a 'contract for services'. This distinction can be viewed as a definition by 'label', that is, what the parties to the contract call themselves. However, labels can be deceptive. For this reason, should there be a dispute over employment or self-employment, or should an individual seek to use the protective employment law available, the court will examine the true nature of the relationship between the parties. The court will look further than the 'labels' attached to each party and will examine in some detail the obligations of the two contracting parties. Only then can employment or self-employment be properly evaluated.

The law does supply a definition of an 'employee' and regards it as an, "individual who has entered into or works under a contract of employment". This will include an apprenticeship. This definition may be quite clear when the individual in question has been issued with a document by his employer entitled, "contract of employment". All too often, however, no such document exists and the position is much less clear. It is within this grey area, where no written contract of employment exists, that the practical definition of employment and self-employment is of most use.

1.3 THE PRACTICAL DEFINITION

The court will look at the reality of the situation and try to ascertain the true relationship between the parties. That said, there is one fundamental requirement in law that must be in place before the court will look further at the relationship. There must be mutual obligations on the 'employer' to provide work for the 'employee' and on the 'employee' personally to perform work for the 'employer'. Where these obligations are present, the court will then take into account the following factors in deciding whether an individual is an employee or not:

- The contractual provisions.
- Does the person work under the orders or control of another?
- Does the person work exclusively for the other party?
- Does the person work as part of the other's business?
- Does the person provide their own plant and equipment?
- Does the person provide their own support staff?
- Is the person responsible for their own profit and loss?
- The arrangements made for the payment of tax, National Insurance contributions, and V.A.T.
- Is the relationship solely designed for tax advantages or to avoid the employment protection legislation?

The list is not exhaustive and no single factor determines the distinction between employment and self-employed status. The test is known as the 'multiple-factor test' and all of the issues are given equal scrutiny. Dealing with the points as they appear above, the following details are helpful.

1.3.1 THE CONTRACTUAL PROVISIONS

This will often be the starting point for the court if a document entitled 'The Contract' or 'The Contract of Employment' etc., is in existence. If it does exist, its intention may be reasonably clear and therefore greatly assist the court. If there is no such documentation the situation is more complex and the court will consider the 'contract' to be the sum of everything agreed orally between the parties and the custom and practice of the parties. This can sometimes be confusing but the explanation is simple. Many people believe that if no written contract or document exists, then there can be no contract. This is not the case in law. Legally a contract may exist between two people without a written document. All the terms of such a contract will be implied and will typically comprise all verbal agreements and working customs between the parties. All of these matters form the 'contract' in the eyes of the law.

1.3.2 WORKING UNDER THE CONTROL OF ANOTHER

A self-employed contractor works to the pre-determined specification and request of another. An employee on the other hand will work under the daily control of another. The control test is not straightforward but generally a self-employed contractor could not be said to be under the constant direction of another. They have to work to guidelines that most often are pre-set and agreed at the commencement of the contract. They are often taken on to perform a specific task and their engagement terminates once that task has been completed.

1.3.3 EXCLUSIVITY

It is a sign of employment where a person works exclusively for one other party. However a self-employed person is free to engage in as many contracts with whomsoever they wish at any time of their choosing. Two or more contracts undertaken at the same time is a traditional hallmark of the self-employed contractor.

1.3.4 WORKING AS PART OF THE BUSINESS

An employee is an integral part of an employer's business and would typically work within the core of a business. For example an employee of a printer would normally work providing some function that assists the core business of printing whether it be sales, administration or printing itself. Conversely, the individual engaged to clean the windows of the print shop twice a week is not in the same sense working as part of the print business. It follows that the window-cleaner in that example is far more likely to be considered self-employed.

1.3.5 PROVISION OF PLANT AND EQUIPMENT

It is usual in the relationship between employer and employee for the employer to provide all the materials, machinery and equipment necessary for the employee to effectively perform their duties. The employee merely turns up for work. A self-employed contractor, however, is more usually under an obligation to provide whatever tools may be necessary to do the job effectively. It is this implied obligation to provide or not to provide their own tools and equipment that is an indicator of employment or self-employment.

1.3.6 SUPPORT STAFF

When a self-employed contractor is asked to perform a particular task, typically it is their responsibility to establish how many people and with what skills, will be necessary to effectively complete that task. The cost of providing such support staff will be borne by the self-employed contractor. An employee, on the other hand, when asked to perform a task will impliedly be able to rely on the employer to provide such support staff as necessary without personal expense.

1.3.7 PROFIT AND LOSS

An independent contractor is indicated where there is a system of payment to an individual in return for work undertaken by that person that involves some element of risk. In the same way that it is not open to an employee to make an increased profit from the way in which he performs his duties. An employee will do good, bad or indifferent work for the same wage. The greater the degree of personal responsibility for profit and loss, the more indicative of self-employment. An independent contractor is in business on his own account and is likely to be paid on invoice.

1.3.8 ARRANGEMENTS FOR TAX AND NATIONAL INSURANCE

A court will consider any such arrangements in place but they will not usually in themselves, prove employment or self-employment. As previously stated, it is the true relationship of the parties which determines their status.

1.3.9 AVOIDANCE OF LEGISLATION

Where a contract is called a 'contract for services' and purports to be self-employed in nature but in applying the above tests, is clearly nothing of the kind, the court will not be fooled. Unscrupulous employers will fail if seeking to use this method to avoid the rigours of employment legislation. Similarly, where an individual has openly requested of another party to be self-employed, for example to reap tax advantages, the court will be wary if that person, when times get hard, claims employment status.

1.3.10 INDICATORS OF EMPLOYMENT
Having applied the above test the following five elements are useful indicators of employment:

- Method of remuneration i.e. by regular wage
  or monthly salary.
- Paid holidays.
- Sick pay provision.
- Provision and availability of a company pension scheme.
- Subjection to disciplinary action in the event of misconduct.

1.4 SPECIFIC RELATIONSHIPS
There are some types of individual who, over the years, have been considered by the courts with regard to their being employees or self-employed. It is useful at this stage to list these types and indicate the court's view on their status.

1.4.1 DIRECTORS
Strictly, a director is not an employee. There need be no contract of employment between a director and the company for which they work. Normally there is a contract called a, "service contract" or, "service agreement". Such contracts will typically include many terms and conditions and although by a different name it is more usually than not deemed by the court to be a contract of employment. This is particularly so where the director is required to perform specific tasks in return for a regular salary.

Most of the cases where a director is not an employee involve small private family companies. A director of such a company may work full-time for that company and not be an employee. The key to the distinction is that a director of a small private company is under far different obligations than their counterpart within a large national organisation.

1.4.2 PARTNERS
Partners are not employees but are self-employed, receiving for payment a share in profits from the business. There is a distinction however between an 'equity partner' and a 'salaried partner'. If the former owns part of the business and therefore takes a share of the profit, that person will be self-employed. A 'salaried partner' does not own a distinct part of the business and receives payment by way of salary only. Such an individual is highly likely to be an employee, being a 'partner' in name only.

1.4.3 HOMEWORKERS

This group of workers are so called due to their working in their own home away from the premises (if any) of the other party. In such situations the court will, once more, look at the true relationship between the parties. That said, the court has decided that home workers who worked flexible terms and dictated when and in what quantity they wanted work were, in fact, employees and entitled to use any protective legislation available to them.

1.4.4 TEMPORARY WORKERS SUPPLIED BY AN AGENCY

For such workers there would normally exist two contracts. One contract between the worker and the agent and another between the agent and the direct recipient of their services (usually the company). In many such arrangements the agent places the worker and pays the worker direct. In most cases of short periods of temporary relief work, such workers will not have a relationship of employment with either the agent or the company with whom they are placed.

The agreement with the agent is regarded as a separate type of contract and quite distinct from one of employment. However, the problem area is the relationship between the worker and the recipient company or other party. Over a period of time it is possible for this relationship to develop into something akin to an employment contract. The usual tests stated earlier in this chapter will be applied. In addition, to add to the confusion, under new legislation agency workers are defined as 'employees' for the purpose of statutory paid annual leave, statutory minimum wage, rest breaks, a limit on average weekly working time to 48 hours (optional) and a limit on night workers' average normal nightly working time to 8 hours. Such legislation is considered to be protective for health and safety reasons, hence the inclusion of agency workers within its remit.

1.5 THE IMPORTANCE OF BEING AN EMPLOYEE

Having discussed in some detail the distinction between employee and self-employed status, it falls now to cover the consequences of recognised employment. Subject to certain qualifying conditions, an employee is entitled to the following rights:

- Protection against unfair dismissal.
- Redundancy pay.
- Notice of termination of employment.
- Guarantee payments in respect of lay-off and short-time working.
- Written particulars of employment.
- Equal pay.
- Maternity rights.
- Protection from race discrimination.
- Protection from sex discrimination.
- Protection from trade union victimisation.
- Time off to fulfil trade union duties.
- To be protected by reasonable health and safety measures.

- Not to have unlawful deductions made from wages.
- To be paid statutory sick pay.
- Protection from discrimination on the grounds of disability.
- National minimum wage.
- Paid annual leave.
- Limitation on working time.
- The right not to be discriminated against on the grounds of religion (Northern Ireland).

All of these rights will be addressed later. With so much at stake, the importance of ascertaining employment status is self-evident.

It should be noted that the Secretary of State will have the power to issue regulations extending individual employment rights to groups of workers not covered by current employment law because they do not technically qualify as "employees". This could encompass a broad range of important employment rights, including those relating to contractual terms, time off work, maternity and parental leave, termination, transfers of undertakings, and working time. It would seem that the Government is committed to ensuring that all workers, other than the genuinely self-employed, enjoy the standards of protection that the existing legislation provides. Home workers and agency workers are specifically mentioned. The enabling power came into force on 25 October 1999 and there will be consultation on the use of this power during the course of year 2000.

1.6 EXCLUDED EMPLOYEES

Even where employment status unquestionably exists, there are circumstances in which employees are denied the benefits of some or all of those rights as listed above. This section will briefly catalogue the main excluded employees.

1.6.1 ILLEGAL CONTRACTS

Any person employed under an illegal contract is not entitled to the protection of the law. This is a matter of public policy. A wrongdoer must not be seen to benefit from their misconduct. A prime example of an illegal contract is one which commits a fraud upon the Inland Revenue. For example where an employee is listed in the 'books' as being paid £100 per week (with tax and National Insurance being paid on that sum) but in fact is given an extra amount of £25 cash-in-hand, this is illegal. Any person receiving payment in a similar fashion will not be entitled to the protection of the employment legislation. Another illegal contract would be where the performance of duties under the contract of employment involve an illegal act. For example, where an employee was required under contract to obtain prostitutes for the customers of his employer.

1.6.2 DIPLOMATIC AND STATE IMMUNITY

In short, in very restricted circumstances, employees of consuls and foreign diplomats residing in this country are excluded from the protection of employment legislation.

1.6.3 CROWN EMPLOYEES

These are employees who work for a government department. Most statutory rights are available to crown employees. The most notable exceptions are the rights to statutory redundancy pay and to a minimum period of notice. Members of the armed forces are crown employees, but are generally not eligible for any statutory rights save race, disability and sex discrimination.

1.6.4 EMPLOYEES OVER THE AGE OF RETIREMENT

For the purposes of this exclusion "over the age of retirement" means:

- Over the age of 65.
- Over the normal retirement age of their employer's business (provided the normal retirement age for that business is the same for both women and men); or where there is no normal retiring age.

Such employees are excluded from claiming statutory redundancy pay and from applying for unfair dismissal before an employment tribunal.

1.6.5 SHORT-TERM AND CASUAL EMPLOYEES

This category of workers is usually excluded from claiming unfair dismissal or statutory redundancy pay because, in practice, they do not obtain the continuous service necessary to bring such actions. That is, one year in respect of unfair dismissal and two years for statutory redundancy pay.

1.6.6 PART-TIME WORKERS

Part-time workers used to be denied the right to claim redundancy payments or unfair dismissal until they had completed five complete years service. This is no longer the case. A House of Lords decision maintained that this unfairly discriminated against women and the five year qualifying period was abandoned. Part-time workers now require two years' continuous service to claim redundancy pay and one year's service to claim unfair dismissal as with full-time workers. Part-time workers have recently been granted additional statutory protection against discrimination in accordance with the European Part-time Work Directive (see section 8.2.15).

1.6.7 EMPLOYMENT OUTSIDE GREAT BRITAIN

In order to seek the protection of British employment rights it follows that the contract of employment must have been made or be applicable in Great Britain. Where an employer is international it is usual for the contract of employment to state quite clearly which country's law will apply in the event of a dispute between the parties. Where the contract is silent and the employee works in and from more than one country the issue of applicable law can be complex. Needless to say, the first issue the court will look at is where the contract was made.

1.6.8 MISCELLANEOUS

Police, share fishermen and merchant seamen are all excluded from claiming unfair dismissal and from receiving a statutory redundancy payment.

1.7 AVOIDING STATUTORY RIGHTS

The statutory rights pertaining to an employee would not be worth the paper they were written on if an employer could insist on excluding such rights by private agreement with the employee. To prevent this, legislation exists making it unlawful for any employer to seek to contract out of statutory rights. Any such agreements, even if signed and agreed by the employee, will be null and void. The most common instance of an employer seeking to avoid statutory rights is not usually seen at the commencement of a contract, but at its end. Many employers will seek to reach an agreement to terminate the contract of employment with the employee. This typically includes a sum of money paid to the employee who in return agrees not to take the matter further before an employment tribunal. To the great surprise of many employers such 'final settlements' are unlawful and they do not prevent the employee from pursuing his rights before an employment tribunal. They will only be lawful if the agreement has been ratified by ACAS (Advisory, Conciliation and Arbitration Service) or complies with strict formal requirements which necessitates an employee having taken independent legal advice before signing any such agreement. Only in this way are the employee's rights properly protected.

1.8 CASE STUDY

Sally is a bookkeeper for ABC Limited. She works 3 days a week and has done so for 5 years. She is responsible for general account keeping, credit control and the payroll. Sally is free to work with whoever she likes on the days of the week she does not work for ABC Limited. In fact, she undertakes no other regular work.

In consideration of Sally's short working week, ABC Limited have always regarded her as self-employed. This is reflected in her tax position which was imposed on Sally at the outset of her association with ABC Limited. Sally is paid monthly after submitting an invoice for her hours worked.

ABC Limited wish to terminate the arrangement with Sally as she is no longer required following the installation of a new computer system in ABC Limited's Accounts Department. Without consultation, Sally is given 4 weeks notice of termination. Sally seeks legal advice and is told the following.

Despite her short hours and tax position, Sally works under the day to day organisation and control of ABC Limited. She attends their offices and uses their equipment and resources. Sally is unable to influence the remuneration she receives for the work she performs. The tax position is not through Sally's choice. In the event Sally is off work due to illness, her pay is maintained. In the circumstances Sally should be regarded, in law, as a part-time employee of ABC Limited. As a result, she is entitled to the statutory minimum period of notice of 5 weeks (one week for each complete year of service, up to a maximum of 12 weeks) and statutory redundancy pay. In addition, because the redundancy was poorly handled by ABC Limited without proper consultation with Sally or any consideration being given to redeployment, she has a possible statutory claim for unfair dismissal.

Sally complains to ABC Limited who are forced to settle the matter with Sally and enhance the terms of severance originally offered.

CHAPTER TWO

THE CONTRACT OF EMPLOYMENT

2.1 FORMATION OF THE CONTRACT

A contract of employment, like any other legal contract, is regulated by basic common law principles. Imposed by statute upon these principles are a number of other legal requirements in respect of the form and content of the contract of employment. For a contract to exist in law between two parties (in this case the employer and the employee) there must be the following elements:

- Offer.
- Acceptance.
- Consideration.

Put simply, that means there must be a clear offer of some sort from the employer of a job to the employee. The employee upon receiving that offer must equally clearly have communicated his acceptance to the employer. And lastly, that the deal was to work for money (consideration) and not to undertake employment as a free volunteer. The offer and acceptance (either or both) may be oral or in writing. There will still be a legal contract between the employer and employee even where no written documentation has changed hands. The importance of written terms and conditions of employment is that should there be a dispute, the contract is easier to prove before a court. In practice, it is common for a job to be offered orally at the end of an interview and to be accepted verbally by the employee. Usually, the employer will formalise the agreement at a later date by issuing the employee with a letter of appointment, expressing the main terms and conditions, or a full contract of employment.

2.2 TERMS OF THE CONTRACT

Just as the contract itself does not have to be in writing, nor do the terms and conditions of that contract. To determine what actually comprises the contract terms in full, courts or tribunals will consider the following types of contract term;

- Express terms.
- Implied terms.
- Incorporated terms.

A contract of employment may, in reality, have some of each type of term, so it is important to be able to recognise the nature of the terms.

2.2.1 EXPRESS TERMS

Such terms may be either written or oral. They may be identified in that they represent what has been specifically agreed between the parties. These terms are usually quite clear and most often confirmed in writing. The importance of express terms is that in law, in the event of a dispute, they will override all other terms of the contract. They have priority.

2.2.2 IMPLIED TERMS

A term may be implied into the contract of employment when its existence is so obvious that it must have been contemplated by the parties even though they did not confirm it specifically in writing. An obvious example is the implication that the employee is to be paid for the work they perform. If the express terms of the contract do not state how much the employee will receive, the court may imply that a reasonable sum of money was to be paid for their work. Other examples of implied terms accepted by the courts in the past include the right to reasonable holiday entitlement and to reasonable notice of termination of the contract to be given to both the employee and the employer. The following common law duties are implied into every contract of employment.

Duty to provide work

This applies where the employee is paid according to what they produce (e.g. piece work). The employer is under a duty to provide work to allow the employee to earn money. In all other situations (non-piece work) the employer is only under the obligation to pay the agreed wage.

Duty to indemnify employees

Where an employee necessarily incurs expense in the performance of their duties, the employer, impliedly, must meet those expenses.

Health and safety

The employer is under a general duty to provide employees with a safe working environment. Employees are doubly protected in this regard since there is also a statutory duty to provide the same. Moreover, employers must, by law, have insurance to cover their liability to employees should they be injured at work. The employer's duty extends to providing safe equipment for the employees' use.

Trust and confidence

The law has determined that every employment relationship requires there to be mutual trust and confidence between the parties. When this trust and confidence is completely undermined by the actions of one party, the contract of employment may be regarded by the other as being at an end. The elements of trust and confidence are another way of expressing the need for respect for each other and co-operation.

Competence

Implied into every contract of employment is that the employee will undertake their work with the required degree of skill and care in order to safely and effectively complete the tasks for which they were employed.

Obeying orders

Employees are under an implied duty to obey reasonable and lawful management instructions. Failure to do so may legitimately lead to dismissal. The instruction will be 'lawful' if it comes from such a person with relevant authority. Whether or not it is 'reasonable' is often open to argument and can be a common area for dispute. As a rule of thumb it will be reasonable if it is either:

- Within the job description in the contract;
- Without being demeaning, is reasonably within the capability of the employee concerned;
- Has been performed by the employee before, without protest.

It follows that where an employee is requested to perform a task which is quite clearly outside of the contract terms, implied or express, the employee will be under no obligation to comply with that request.

Faithfulness

Sometimes referred to as the 'duty of fidelity', in essence, this is the implied duty to work in good faith for the employer and not to engage in work for another or for oneself that may compete with, or damage, the employer's business. An employee should not be able to make a personal profit by breaching the duty of good faith to the detriment of their employer. It follows that if an employee was to 'moonlight' in competition with the employer's business, the duty of faithfulness would undoubtedly be breached bringing the contract of employment to an end. That said, 'moonlighting' in some capacity unrelated to the business of the main employer is unlikely to effect the relationship of good faith between the parties.

Confidentiality

In most employment relationships the employee will, from time to time, come into possession of commercial information which is by its nature confidential. To disclose it could damage the employer's business. For example, if lists of clients and their terms of business with the employer were to fall into the hands of a competitor, great financial damage could be caused to the employer. Therefore, implied into every contract of employment is a duty on the employee not to disclose obviously confidential information to a third party. Breach of this duty could, once more, bring about the termination of the contract of employment if the employer so desired.

Not all information is protected by this implied term. During employment protected confidential information is not necessarily restricted to 'trade secrets' a wider category of information may be protected. Post-termination of the contract of employment only that information which by its nature is a 'trade secret' and patently confidential is protected. In fact, much of the information an employee is given during their employment falls outside of this category of confidential material. In trying to distinguish between the confidential information caught by the implied term and that which is not, the following guidelines are often used by the courts:

- Has the employer made it clear to the employee that particular information was to be regarded as confidential?
- Is the confidential information in question readily distinguished from other general information in respect of an employer?
- Would a third party have an alternative means of legitimately accessing the information other than being told by the employee?
- The nature of the employment will be examined including the status and responsibility of the employee concerned and the frequency with which they dealt with such information.

Finally, on this section dealing with implied terms, it is possible for a term to be implied into the contract through custom and practice. That is, although there is no verbal or written agreement between the parties, the employer or employee, through habit, so act that their conduct becomes an implied term of the contract. There are many examples. One, typically, would be where a van driver as a matter of fact, always drives the company vehicle home at night and back to work in the morning even though no express permission has been given by the employer. After a period of time, usually months not weeks, this custom and practice will become a term and condition (an employee's right) under the contract. In practice, much depends on the custom itself and the period of time over which the conduct has taken place. Each 'acquired' implied term will ultimately depend on the particular facts of each case.

2.2.3 INCORPORATED TERMS

The prime example of an incorporated term is one that becomes part of an employee's contract by reason of it being negotiated by a trade union with the employer on behalf of the employee (or usually group of employees). The agreement is not made directly between the two parties to the contract, the employee and employer, but by a third party – the union. In law, the unions can only negotiate terms which may be incorporated into the employee's individual contract if it:

1. Has the right to negotiate with the employer, that is, is recognised by the employer for the purposes of collective bargaining; and
2. The matter to which the negotiations relate is within one of the following categories and relates to:

- Terms and conditions of employment.
- The physical conditions of employment.
- Engagement, non-engagement, termination or suspension of employment.
- Allocation of work.
- Discipline.
- Membership or non-membership of a trade union.
- Facilities for trade union officials.
- Facilities for negotiations or consultation in relation to any of the above matters.

2.3 STATUTORY REQUIREMENTS

The law does not require an employer to issue the employee with a 'contract of employment' as such. Instead, the employer is under a statutory obligation to issue what is called 'written particulars of employment'. Moreover, these written particulars must be issued to the employee within one month from the commencement of employment. The written statement must state the following:

- The name of the employer and employee.
- The date upon which employment commenced.
- The date upon which the employee's period of continuous service began, whether or not different from the date upon which employment commenced.
- The rate of pay and interval between payments (weekly/monthly etc.).
- Hours of work.
- Holiday entitlement, holiday pay and the rate of accrual.
- Sickness/injury pay or entitlement.
- Pension entitlement and whether a contracting-out certificate is in force in respect of any occupational pension scheme in place – statements must be provided even if the employer makes no provision over and above the state pension scheme.
- The length of notice which the employee is entitled to give and to receive in order that the contract of employment may be terminated.
- Job title.
- The employee's place of work (or, if variable, the employer's address).
- If the employment is temporary, the time period of that intended employment.
- If the contract is for a fixed period of time, the date upon which that fixed-term contract will end.
- Any collective agreement which may affect the terms and conditions of employment.

Where the employee is required to work outside the U.K. for more than one month, the written statement must provide the following information:

- The period of working outside the U.K.
- The currency of remuneration.
- Any additional remuneration and benefits.
- Any terms and conditions relating to the employee's return to the U.K.
- Any disciplinary rules applicable to the employee.
- A person to whom the employee may complain if dissatisfied with any disciplinary decision.
- A person to whom the employee may complain if they wish to raise a grievance in respect of any aspect of their employment.

Where an employer has less than 20 employees on the date that the employee started employment, there is no obligation to provide disciplinary rules. The only obligation is to identify the person to whom the employee may raise a grievance.

2.3.1 THE PARTIES NAMES

Both employer and employee must be named. This is particularly important where there has been a change of employer, for example following a recent takeover of a business.

2.3.2 THE DATE EMPLOYMENT COMMENCED

For the purpose of seeking the protection of some of the employment legislation provisions (as discussed later) it is necessary, particularly where an employee may have re-joined an employer after a short break elsewhere, to ascertain the starting point for that subsequent period of employment and whether it may be added to a previous period of service for the purpose of calculating continuous service.

2.3.3 PAY

All details of remuneration should be clearly stated, including bonus and commission payments, shift premiums and benefits in kind such as luncheon vouchers where applicable. The pay interval must be stated.

Pay cannot be less than the current national minimum wage. That is £3.00 per hour for 18-21 year olds (rising to £3.20 per hour from 1st June 2000), £3.60 per hour for workers aged 22 and above (rising to £3.70 per hour from 1st October 2000) and £3.20 per hour for workers doing accredited training. No benefits in kind (such as the provision of meals) count towards the national minimum wage, except accommodation in respect of which the amount that can count towards the national minimum wage must not be greater than £19.95 per week. Tips only count if they go through the payroll.

2.3.4 HOURS OF WORK

This should include details of the core working hours of the week and within what times of the day they should be worked. Lunch times and other breaks should be stated along with details of overtime where applicable, such as the rate of pay and whether it is voluntary or compulsory. The right to lay-off staff in periods of work shortage should also be detailed in this section of the written particulars along with any contractual right to vary the hours of work upon issuing reasonable notice of the change to the employee concerned.

An employee need not work more than an average of 48 hours per week but has a free choice to do so if they wish. In such circumstances, the right to limit hours of work to 48 per week will need to be expressly waived. The employer should prepare an appropriate document for the employee to sign. The standard averaging period is 17 weeks or the period worked to date if the employee has been employed less then 17 weeks. The employer is under no obligation to keep appropriate records of weekly hours worked but it may be good practice to do so. An employee is entitled to an uninterrupted break of 20 minutes when the daily working time is more than 6 hours. The break may be paid or unpaid and this is subject to agreement between the employer and employee. An adolescent employee (over compulsory school leaving age but under 18 years old) is entitled to a rest break of 30 minutes when the daily working time is more than 4½ hours. The rest break should not be at the beginning or the end of the working periods stated above. The entitlement to a rest break does not apply to employees in a range of circumstances:

- Where an employee's activities are such that his place of work and place of residence are distant from one another or his different places of work are distant from one another.
- Where an employee is 'engaged in security and surveillance activities', i.e., where there is a need for a round-the-clock presence.
- Where an employee's activities include the need for continuity of service or production, i.e., hospitals, residential institutions, prisons, docks, airports, press, radio, television, postal services, gas, water and electricity production, agriculture etc.
- Where there is a foreseeable surge of activity, i.e., agriculture, tourism and postal services.
- Where an employee's activities are affected by an occurrence due to unusual and unforeseeable circumstances, or exceptional events, the consequences of which could not have been avoided, or an accident, or the imminent risk of an accident. In these circumstances, the employee is entitled to 'an equivalent period of compensatory rest'.

2.3.5 NIGHT WORK LIMITS

An employer is required to take all reasonable steps to ensure that the normal hours of their night workers do not exceed an average of 8 hours for each 24 hours over a 17 week period. The averaging period may be extended in certain circumstances. Night-time is a period of at least 7 hours which includes the period from midnight to 5am which can be determined by a relevant agreement (for example, 10pm to 5am or 12pm to 7am). In the absence of such an agreement it will be 11pm to 6am.

A 'night worker' is any worker whose daily working time includes at least three hours of night time:

- On the majority of days they work.
- On such a proportion of the days they work as is agreed between the employer and the workers in a collective or workforce agreement; or
- Sufficiently often that they may be said to work such hours as a normal course.

2.3.6 HOLIDAYS

This section should include the number of days entitlement, the rate of pay, the rate of accrual and entitlement (if any) to public or bank holidays. Employees should be aware that, contrary to popular belief, there is no statutory right to take public or bank holidays let alone to be paid for them! There is, however, a statutory right to a minimum of four weeks paid leave per year for all employees. This leave includes the eight statutory bank holidays. Employees become entitled to four weeks paid leave after thirteen weeks of service. The entitlement will accrue on a month to month basis and after thirteen weeks is calculated from the commencement of employment. Part-timers are entitled to a proportionate amount of leave in accordance with hours worked. Where a part-timer works variable hours an average is taken over the previous 12 weeks worked.

2.3.7 SICK PAY

Should the employee be sick or injured the particulars should state what their entitlements are, whether that is reference only to the provisions of the statutory sick pay (SSP) scheme or that the employer pays a contractual amount above the basic entitlement. There should also be available full details of the rules for qualifying for SSP or other sick pay scheme and for how long such payments will be made and whether any amount paid over and above SSP is a contractual entitlement, or at the discretion of the employer.

2.3.8 PENSIONS

Details of any company pension scheme must be provided and whether the employer is contracted in or out of the state pension scheme.

2.3.9 NOTICE PERIOD

The written statement of particulars must provide details of notice required to terminate the contract. However, it must never be less than the statutory minimum requirement that states that the employer must give the employee the following periods of notice dependant upon length of service:

- Less than one months service – a reasonable period of notice (which may be less than one week).

- Between one months and two years service – 1 weeks' notice.
- Between 2 years and 12 years service – 1 week for each complete year of service.
- Over 12 years service – 12 weeks' notice.

The employee, on the other hand, must give the employer at least one week's notice where he has one months service or more, but this does not increase with the length of service. Both parties to the contract of employment may agree to a different period of notice than the statutory amount. However, it must never be less than that amount as stated above.

2.3.10 JOB TITLE

This should adequately and appropriately describe the job duties the employee is required to undertake. It is quite lawful for the employer to keep this broad and add such phrases as, "… and to perform any other duties reasonably within your capability and skills as the interests of the business dictate". A job description or title is most often a combination of what is expressed within the contract or written statement of particulars and what the employee does in practice.

2.3.11 TEMPORARY EMPLOYMENT

The requirement to be issued with a written statement of terms and conditions of employment applies equally to temporary employees as it does to permanent, provided always that the temporary contract of employment is to last more than one month.

2.3.12 DISCIPLINARY RULES

Small employers, those who employ less than 20 members of staff are given some latitude by the legislation. They do not have to provide details of disciplinary rules and procedures. However, where they exist as a matter of practice, a note specifying what the procedure is, or referring to a document which contains it, must be included within the statement.

2.3.13 GRIEVANCES

The statement of particulars should provide details of who to complain to and the procedure for complaining stating:

- In what form, oral or written, the grievance should be made.
- The time period in which the grievance will be considered by the employer.
- Whose decision is final.
- How and when that final decision will be communicated.

Finally, it should be noted that the content of the written statement of particulars is the bare minimum statutory requirement. A good employer will go far beyond this statement, adding and clarifying many other terms and conditions of employment. A good contract of employment is a source of reference for both employee and employer, in the event of a disputed term or condition.

2.4 STATUTORY TERMS AFFECTING THE CONTRACT OF EMPLOYMENT

2.4.1 THE EQUAL PAY ACT 1970

Implied into every woman's contract of employment is the right to pay equal to that of a man where the woman undertakes work that is:

- Like work to a man.
- Work rated as equivalent to work done by a man.
- Work of equal value to that done by a man.

The provisions of the Act were designed deliberately to combat the problem of discrimination in pay between the sexes but does in fact apply equally to men as well as to women. The right to equal pay will operate on the contract of employment in that any term relating to pay which is unequal will be modified so as to provide equality.

Such claims for equal pay may be defended only on the ground that the variation between a woman's and a man's contract is genuinely due to a material factor which is not the difference of sex. The law in this area can be complex and it is sufficient for the purposes of this volume to state that the law requires such material factors, where they are alleged to exist, to be objectively justified by the employer.

A claim for equal pay may be brought before an employment tribunal and, if successful, the amount awarded will be the difference in pay between that of the claimant and the 'equivalent' employee. Arrears of up to two years pay may be recovered by this process.

2.4.2 DISCRIMINATION

Implied by statute into every contract of employment is the making unlawful of any discrimination on the grounds of:

- Sex.
- Marital status.
- Colour.
- Race.
- Nationality.
- Ethnic origin.
- National origin.
- Disability (where the employer has 15 or more employees).
- Religion (Northern Ireland).

Discrimination is discussed in detail later in Chapter 8.

2.4.3 HEALTH AND SAFETY AT WORK

Broadly, legislation in respect of health and safety impacts on the contract of employment in providing that certain standards must be maintained by the employer. The employee has the right:

- To enjoy generally a healthy and safe place of work.
- To be protected by the employer from risks to their health and safety arising out of or in connection with their work.
- To be protected from substances hazardous to health that are used or kept at the work place. (See later in Chapter 12)

2.4.4 PATENTS ACT 1977
This Act covers the inventions of employees whilst in the course of work and clarifies ownership of that item or substance in law. Inventions generally belong to the employer where:

- The invention was made during the employee's normal duties.
- The employee had a particular responsibility or special obligation to further the interests of the employer's business.

2.4.5 COPYRIGHT, DESIGNS AND PATENTS ACT 1988
This is similar in application to section 2.4.4 above, but deals with the copyright of literary, musical or dramatic works rather than a particular item or substance in tangible form.

2.4.6 EMPLOYER'S LIABILITY (COMPULSORY INSURANCE) ACT 1969
Implied into every contract of employment is the obligation on the employer to have adequate insurance in the event of personal injury (including industrial disease) being inflicted on the employee during the course of their employment duties arising out of the employer's negligence or breach of statutory duty.

2.4.7 FACTORIES ACT 1961
This Act implies duties on the factory employer in respect of:

- Cleanliness.
- Working temperature.
- Ventilation.
- Lighting.
- Safe machinery.

2.4.8 OFFICES, SHOPS AND RAILWAY PREMISES ACT 1963
Similar to section 2.4.7 above but applicable to many more smaller working environments.

2.4.9 EMPLOYER'S LIABILITY (DEFECTIVE EQUIPMENT) ACT 1969
An employer is under an implied duty to pay damages to any employee injured as a result of using defective equipment provided by the employer, whilst in the normal course of their employment.

2.4.10 EMPLOYMENT RIGHTS ACT 1996

Under this Act the employee has the right in certain circumstances not to have deductions made from their wages. The subject of deductions is dealt with in detail in Chapter 3.

2.5 TERMS NOT CONSIDERED TO BE CONTRACTUAL

The content of this chapter has been dedicated to terms and conditions which are considered to form part of the contract of employment whether express, implied, or incorporated via collective agreement or statutory requirement or obligation. To complete the picture, it should be noted that some terms will not always be considered contractual.

Many employers provide policy statements which may cover many matters such as carrying out routine work, not smoking on the employer's premises, or the procedures to be adopted in the event of redundancy. Policy statements dealing with these matters will not always be contractual. Much will depend on the facts of any particular case. The importance of their status as non-contractual is that if breached by employer or employee, the aggrieved party may have no legal redress.

It is often difficult to tell whether such policy statements are intended to form part of the body of the contract of employment. A key indictor of contractual status is the indication of disciplinary sanction against the employee in the event of breach. Other than that, there is often no simple solution and the court will arrive at its decision by setting the policy statement in the context of other documentation and the custom and practice of that particular place of work.

2.6 CASE STUDY

Mandy is an office manager working for Wiseguys Pizzas Limited. She is paid monthly. She has never been issued with a written statement of the main terms and conditions of employment. After a 10 week probationary period Mr Paccino, her manager, dismisses Mandy telling her to leave the premises immediately. Mr Paccino does not pay Mandy any notice money. Mandy seeks legal advice.

Mandy is entitled to a statutory minimum period of notice of 1 week. This must be paid in lieu if Mr Paccino does not want her to work it. Because Mandy is paid monthly, is a senior employee and there is no written agreement in respect of notice upon termination of the contract, she may reasonably imply she is entitled to one months' notice of termination in line with her pay period. Mandy is not entitled to any accrued holiday pay having less than 13 weeks' service.

CHAPTER THREE
PAY

3.1 FORM OF PAYMENT

By virtue of legislation that took effect from 1987, manual workers no longer have the right to be paid in cash or "coin of the realm" as it was known. The method and form of payment is now a matter of private agreement between the employer and the employee. However, there remains a great number of manual workers who are still paid cash. For those workers there now seems little doubt that, provided their employer gives reasonable notice and has some business reason for the change, they may impose a cashless pay system. That is, one in which a credit transfer is made into the bank account of the employee concerned at a regular interval.

Technically, if an employer were to forcibly impose a cashless pay system on a previously cash-paid employee, this could constitute a breach of contract. It seems that courts would not be inclined to award anything other than nominal damages in such cases, in particular where the employer provides some business reason for the change, for example an efficiency or security reason.

3.2 ITEMISED PAY STATEMENT

Employees have a legal right to an itemised pay statement unless they are:

- Engaged in Police service.
- Employed as a share fisherman or merchant seaman.

The pay statements must contains the following details:

- The gross amount of wage or salary.
- The net amount of wage or salary.
- Amounts of (and reasons for) any variable or fixed deductions.
- Where different parts of the net amount are paid in different ways, the amount and method of payment of each part payment.

It is a further requirement that the statement be given to the employee on or before the date pay is normally due under the contract. In respect of fixed deductions the following information is required:

- A cumulative statement of aggregate fixed deductions.
- The amount of the deduction.
- The interval at which it was made.
- The purpose for which it was made.

A statement of fixed deductions may be amended by the employer by notice in writing to the employee containing details of the amendment. A standing statement of fixed deductions will only remain effective for twelve months after which time the employer must re-issue the statement, with any amendments.

Should an employee believe that their pay statement is incorrect, incomplete in any way, or non-existent, their remedy ultimately is to take the matter before an employment tribunal for compensation or a declaration as to their rights. If the employment tribunal finds that deductions were made which were not properly notified, it can order the employer to reimburse the employee the amount of any such un-notified deductions made in the 13 weeks immediately before the employee lodged the complaint.

3.3 DEDUCTIONS FROM WAGES

In the mid 1980's legislation was introduced to protect employees from rogue employers who claimed-back large sums of money by way of a range of deductions from their wage for various reasons. Often deductions were made without notice to the employee and for reasons far from clear, let alone agreed by the employee concerned. A statutory framework for regulating deductions only in certain circumstances is now contained in the Employment Rights Act 1996. The Act covers most but not all forms of deduction. Excluded from the provision are those deductions made:

- To facilitate reimbursement to the employer of a previous overpayment of wages.
- Further to a statutory provision (e.g. tax, National Insurance contributions).
- As a result of any disciplinary proceedings made under any statutory provision.
- Where the employer is bound by statute to deduct and pay over an amount to a public authority (e.g. an attachment of earnings order within the County Court System).
- To pay a third person where the employee consents in writing to such payment and the third person has notified the employer of that amount (e.g. a payment to a private pension company).
- Further to the employee's participation in a strike or other industrial action and the deduction relates to this action.
- Further to the satisfaction of an order of a court or tribunal for the payment of an amount by the employee to the employer.

Other than these exclusions, the general rule is that any deduction from the wage of an employee will be unlawful unless the employee has given the employer prior written consent to make that deduction. Any deduction made unlawfully will afford the employee the right to take the matter before an employment tribunal to reclaim the sum involved and to have the deduction declared unlawful. The practical effect of having the deduction declared unlawful is important, since its effect is to prevent the employer from recovering that sum through any other legal channels even if there was a good case for arguing a right to recovery. For example, if an employer gives a loan to an employee and the employee fails to repay on time, to deduct the amount (or any part) of that loan from the employee's wages without prior written consent will be unlawful. If declared unlawful by a tribunal the employer will, in effect, be penalised for the unlawful deduction by being barred from recovering the loan by any other court action.

Furthermore, "prior written consent" means exactly what it says. Any written consent of the employee obtained after the deduction has been made will be unlawful. In addition, the consent must precede not only the deduction itself but also the event or conduct giving rise to the deduction. Any contractual provision must be in writing and clearly indicate that in particular circumstances a sum may be deducted from the employee's wage.

3.3.1 THE DEFINITION OF 'WAGE'

Wages, for the purposes of this statutory provision, will include the following sums payable to the worker:

* Fees.
* Bonus payments.
* Commission.
* Holiday pay.
* Statutory sick pay.
* Statutory maternity pay.
* Guarantee payments (in respect of lay-off - see later in this chapter).
* Any sums ordered to be paid by an employment tribunal for reinstatement/re-engagement (see Chapter 4).
* Earned overtime.
* Basic wage or salary.

'Wage' does not include:

* An advance under a loan agreement or an advance of wages.
* Expenses.
* Pension payments.
* A compensatory payment for loss of office.
* Redundancy payments.
* Other payments that may have been made to the employee but were done so in some capacity other than that of an employer and employee relationship.
* A non-contractual payment in lieu of notice.

3.3.2 RETAIL WORKERS

Special provisions apply to workers within the retail industry in respect of cash shortages and stock deficiencies. The maximum deduction on any pay day must not exceed 10% of the gross wages on that day. This ceiling figure of 10% will not apply to a retail worker's final wage or salary. In order to put into effect this right to deduct money from a retail worker's pay the employer must:

- Inform the employee, in writing, of their total liability to the employer in respect of stock shortages or deficiency.
- Make a written demand for payment that is on a pay day.

The demand can be made on the first pay day after written notification to the employee. However, generally shortages and deficiencies which occurred at some time before the last 12 months up to the point of demand are not recoverable by the employer.

3.3.3 REMEDY

An employee must take his complaint of an unlawful deduction from wages before an employment tribunal. The claim must be made within 3 months of the date of deduction. Where a series of allegedly unlawful deductions have been made the 3 month period will run from the date of the last deduction. The employment tribunal has the authority to declare the deduction unlawful and to order the employer to make a repayment to the employee.

3.4 ATTACHMENT OF EARNINGS

An attachment of earnings order is one made by a court in favour of a creditor over a debtor-employee. The order operates by instructing the employer of the debtor-employee to pay a sum of money at a regular interval directly to the court office. This sum of money payable is taken from the wage or salary owed by the employer to the debtor-employee. Such payments are typically ordered by the court in respect of the following matters:

- Child support.
- Maintenance for the employee's ex-wife or common law wife.
- Judgment debts (provided they are for more than £50).
- Payments under an administration order (in the case of a series of debts being owed to various creditors).
- Criminal fines further to a conviction.
- Payment under a legal aid contribution order.

Under an attachment of earnings order the employer is under a legal obligation to make the requested deduction and forward it to the court. Certain provisions exist to limit the amount that may be deducted from the employee's wage. The definition of 'earnings' which may be subject to attachment is wide and includes:

- Wages.
- Salary.
- Bonuses.
- Commission.

- Overtime payments.
- Certain pension payments.

These payments are known as the 'attachable earnings'. In order to ascertain the amount to be deducted, known as the 'normal deduction', the court must first assess what level of earnings the employee requires for his basic needs. The amount required for such needs is the 'protected earnings' of the employee and no deduction can be made which would leave the employee with any less than the protected earnings amount.

More than one attachment of earnings order may be made against an employee at any one time. Priority will be given to the orders chronologically. Faced with an attachment of earnings order the employer must comply or risk a conviction and fine. In addition, the employer may charge the employee, by way of a deduction from the wage, a small sum of money to cover the administration cost of each deduction made. Notice of this deduction must be given in writing to the employee.

3.5 STATUTORY GUARANTEE PAYMENTS

An employee has the right to receive a statutory guarantee payment from their employer if work is not provided by the employer due to:

- A reduction in the employer's business which affects the work of the employee.
- Some other occurrence that affects the employer's business and in turn the work of the employee.

An example of the first point would be a reduction in business orders due to the economic conditions in a particular market. The second is designed to cover situations such as a power cut.

In order to be eligible for the payment the employee must have been employed for one month before the first day without work and must not be working under a fixed term contract of three months or less. In addition, the employee must not unreasonably refuse to undertake other similar duties within their capability if requested by the employer, in an attempt to find suitable alternative work for the employee. What is 'reasonable' is a matter of degree but there will be an obligation on the employee not to be deliberately obstructive.

> The maximum amount payable is £16.10 per day for the first 5 workless days in any 3 month period. Less than £16.10 may only be paid if the employee would normally earn under that figure per day.

If the employee is normally required to work less than 5 days a week, the entitlement cannot exceed the number of days the employee is required to work per week under their contract.

It is important to note in this section that an employer does not have any right to lay off employees unless such a right exists in the contract of employment. This means that where the right exists the employer can simply enforce the statutory guarantee payment system as the needs of the business dictates. Where the right does not exist, in order to reduce pay by any amount at all, the employer must actively seek the agreement of those employees to be affected. Since, to impose a reduction in pay or guarantee pay itself where no right to lay off exists, without the agreement of the employee, will be to act in breach of contract. Should the employers fail to make a guarantee payment the employee's redress would be an application for payment to an employment tribunal, made within 3 months of the day for which a guarantee payment is claimed.

3.6 THE INSOLVENT EMPLOYER

It is an unfortunate fact of life that, occasionally, an employer may be forced out of business due to economic circumstances. When this does occur it often leaves many employees who are owed pay of one kind or another. Some pay is owed under the contract of employment, e.g. arrears in wages and accrued holiday entitlement. Others are statutory rights, e.g. notice and redundancy payments. In assessing the employees' rights in this respect, the starting point is the legal priority in which payments will be made to the employer's creditors. The 'pecking order' is as follows:

- Secured creditors e.g. the Inland Revenue or institutions (usually banks) which have lent money to the employer on the security of particular assets.
- Preferred creditors. Employees are said to have a 'preferential' debt owed to them.
- Ordinary creditors, those not secured or preferred but nonetheless are owed money by the employer, e.g. a supplier of materials to the employer's business.
- Deferred creditors, e.g. a person or institution that lent the employer money in return for a share of the profits.

When the employer is bankrupt or, if a limited company, made insolvent, the assets of the employer are disposed of. Any money made by this disposal is then given to the creditors in strict prioritised order. In practice, many ordinary and deferred creditors, being down the list, receive only a fraction of what is actually owed to them. The employee, as a preferred creditor, is entitled to receive the following provided there are funds left after the secured creditors have been paid:

- All wages and salary for up to 4 months immediately prior to insolvency (including statutory sick pay and statutory guarantee payments).
- All accrued holiday entitlement up to the date of termination of the contract of employment by reason of the employer's insolvency.

In any event, any sum payable relating to the points above is subject to a maximum of £800 per employee. It is evident therefore that the "preferred debtor" provisions can prove harsh. For this reason, certain debts are guaranteed to be paid by the State where the employer has no money to make the payments owed. The following guaranteed debts are recoverable:

- Pay arrears for up to eight weeks subject to a maximum amount of £230 per week. (This will include commission due, overtime payments etc.).
- Accrued holiday entitlement up to six weeks subject to a maximum of £230 per week.
- Employment tribunal basic award if dismissal by the employer was proven to be unfair.
- The statutory minimum period of notice (one week for each complete year of service up to a maximum of twelve weeks) subject to a maximum of £230 per week.
- Apprentices and articled clerks are entitled to reimbursement of their fees.
- Statutory maternity pay.
- Redundancy payments.

In the case of unpaid pension contributions by the insolvent employer, special provisions apply for the State to make such payments and to determine the amount payable. If an employee feels they have not been paid their full preferred and guaranteed entitlements, they may apply to an employment tribunal for determination as to precisely how much is due.

3.7 THE RIGHT TO PAYMENT DURING NOTICE

Where an employee tells their employer that they are leaving but are not ready or willing to work their notice period, they will not be entitled to any payment in lieu of notice. They will only be entitled to pay up to and including their last day of work. However, where they do offer notice to the employer but they are not wanted or they fall sick during the period of notice, the employee will be entitled to the statutory period of notice to be paid by the employer at their normal rate of pay. This will be simple to calculate where the employee receives a normal rate of pay. Where a week's pay varies according to the amount of work done, there exists a formula for calculating a 'week's pay'.

Where pay is variable, a week's pay is calculated as being the average hourly rate multiplied by the number of normal working hours in a week. The average hourly rate is calculated by referring to the period of 12 weeks immediately preceding the first day of the notice period where there are normal working hours. The average hourly rate is based on the hours actually worked by the employee (including overtime) and on the money they were paid for those hours. If there should be no normal working hours, a week's pay is the average weekly pay over the last 12 weeks before the first day of notice.

3.8 STATUTORY SICK PAY

Statutory sick pay, or SSP as it is known, must be distinguished from other forms of sick pay that may be payable under an individual's contract of employment. SSP is the minimum amount of sick pay that all employees are entitled to (subject to qualification). If eligible, the employer must pay the employee this amount of sick pay. In a great number of cases the employer will, as a benefit to the employee, pay over the SSP amount and anything up to the full rate of pay for periods of sickness. Such a payment will be payable under the contract. This section deals with SSP only. Those employees not entitled to SSP are:

- Employees aged 65 or over on the first day of sickness.
- Employees under a fixed term contract of three months or less.
- Those employees who earn (currently) less than £67 per week. Known as the 'lower earnings limit'.
- Employees who go sick within 8 weeks or 52 weeks of having received certain social security benefits.
- Those who have performed no work for the employer under the contract of employment.
- Employees who are off sick during a stoppage at work due to a trade dispute (unless that employee can prove no direct interest in that dispute).
- Employees who are pregnant and go off sick during the maternity pay period (see Chapter 10).
- Those who have already been due 28 weeks SSP from their employer(s) in any one period of incapacity for work (or any two or more 'linked' periods, i.e. separated by 8 weeks or less period of entitlement of 3 years – see 3.8.1).
- Employees who have already been due 28 weeks of SSP from a previous employer and on joining a new employer and again going sick, the gap between the period of incapacity is 8 weeks or less.
- Employees in legal custody on the first day of incapacity.

Provided none of the above exclusions apply the requirements for qualification are that the employee:

- Must have 4 or more consecutive days of sickness (including non-work days and holidays) during which they are too ill to work.
- Must notify the employer of their absence.
- Must supply evidence of the incapacity, commonly:

1. A self-certificate for the period of 4 to 7 calendar days;
2. A doctor's certificate of illness from the 8th day of sickness onwards.

3.8.1 THE PAYMENT PERIOD

The period of sickness of 4 days or more is called the 'period of incacity for work' (PIW). Two or more PIW's which are separated by eight weeks or less are said to be 'linked' and are counted as one PIW. During a PIW, SSP is payable only:

- Where there is a period of entitlement, and
- For the days within the PIW which are 'qualifying days'.

3.8.2 QUALIFYING DAYS
SSP is only paid in respect of 'qualifying days' which will usually be the days in which the employee is normally at work. If the normal working days are Monday to Friday, they will be the qualifying days.

3.8.3 WORKING DAYS
SSP is not payable for the first 3 qualifying days in the period of entitlement. It is the 4th day of sickness which triggers the SSP entitlement. Payment will only be made from the 4th day (including that day) onwards.

PIWs can be linked where they are not separated by more than 56 calendar days. Where they are linked there are no waiting days for the second period of incapacity. For example, an employee who is off for 2 weeks comes back to work for a month and then goes off for a further 5 days. They will receive SSP for the second PIW of 5 days because it is linked in time with the first. Absences of less than 4 days do not constitute a PIW and no SSP is payable.

3.8.4 PERIODS OF ENTITLEMENT
SSP is currently payable for a maximum of 28 weeks. This need not be a single period but could be a series of linked PIWs within a maximum period of entitlement of 3 years. Once the 28 weeks has been exhausted the employee must look to the State for any sickness benefit.

3.8.5 SSP RATES
The rate of SSP depends on the employee's average gross weekly earnings during the 8 weeks preceding the PIW. Rates are reviewed annually and currently stand at £60.20 per week for a maximum of 28 weeks. Maximum SSP payable is, therefore, £1685.60.

3.8.6 LEAVER'S STATEMENT
When an employee's contract of employment comes to an end the employer must issue a leaver's statement (Form SSP1(L)). A new employee should give his leaver's statement to the new employer. If the employee falls sick within the first 8 weeks of new employment the information on the statement may affect the employee's entitlement to SSP.

3.8.7 WITHHOLDING SSP
SSP may be withheld by the employer if they have reason to believe that the employee was not ill or failed to comply with the employer's notification of absence procedure. The employer may set rules in

respect of notification, providing they are reasonable. Where SSP is withheld the employee has the right to request a written statement from the employer specifying the days on which SSP was and was not paid and in respect of the latter the reason for non-payment.

If the employer feels SSP has been unreasonably withheld they may make a complaint to an Inland Revenue adjudication officer. The officer will ask both parties to provide written observations before he makes his formal decision and the officer hearing the appeal will try to decide it by agreement between the employer, the employee and the original officer. If all parties are unable to agree, the appeal will be considered by the Tax Commissioners.

3.9 OVERPAYMENT OF WAGES OR SALARY

There are two types of mistaken overpayment:

1. A mistake of fact.
2. A mistake of law.

Mistakes of law are not easy to determine (even for the courts) and involve the interpretation and construction of contract or statute. In truth, this difficult deliberation is not often necessary since most mistaken overpayments are mistakes of fact. Clerical errors, miscalculations, wrong data input and computer errors are all mistakes of fact.

It follows that should an employee receive an overpayment in their wage packet, it is likely to be recoverable by the employer if they find out. Spending the overpayment will not provide the employee with a legal defence! There may be genuine occasions where the employee unknowingly receives an overpayment by way of clerical error. This, as said, will be recoverable. If the error has taken place over many months the employee could have received a considerable amount and have spent some or all of the money involved. In such cases, it would be unreasonable for the employer to demand repayment in a lump sum and the employee should seek to negotiate an agreeable staged repayment.

The only legal defence open to an employee in receipt of a mistaken overpayment is if they can persuade the court that in good faith they changed their position and incurred expenditure which would not otherwise have been incurred. The 'good faith' element of this defence is important, as it implies that the employee did not know, nor should they reasonably have known, that they were being overpaid.

3.10 EQUAL PAY

The provisions of the Equal Pay Act 1970 require equal pay for 'equal work' regardless of the employee's sex. The right to equal pay applies to:

*   Women employed in Great Britain whether or not they are British citizens; and,
*   Men as well as women.

In practice, most cases under the provisions are brought by women, which is reflected in the remainder of this section.

3.10.1 THE EQUALITY CLAUSE
The Act provides that an 'equality clause' is impliedly included into a woman's contract of employment where one does not already exist. The clause operates so that:

*   A term that is less favourable is modified to become as favourable as that within a corresponding man's contract.
*   Any beneficial term in a man's contract but not in a corresponding woman's will be deemed to include that term.

3.10.2 THE COMPARISON
The woman can compare herself with a man employed by the same or an associated employer if:

*   They do 'like work'; or
*   A job-evaluation scheme has rated their work as equivalent; or
*   Her job is of equal value.

A woman may be regarded as employed on like work with men if her work and theirs is of the same or of a broadly similar nature. This means that any difference that may exist between the two roles are not of practical importance. The work must be 'like work'. The woman cannot claim, for example, if her work involved greater responsibility or skill but was less well paid.

With regard to a job-evaluation study, it must be remembered that the employer is under no legal duty to conduct such a study. However, where they do and a woman's work is rated equivalent to that of a man's by considering effort, skill, qualifications and responsibilities etc. this will facilitate an equal pay claim.

If the work is not 'like work' and no job-evaluation study has been conducted, the woman may bring an equal pay claim if she can show that her work is of 'equal value' to that of a corresponding male. The question of equal value requires assessment of skill, effort, responsibilities etc. just as with a job-evaluation study. Importantly, recent case law also suggests that a woman may bring an equal value claim where the work she is doing is, in fact, of greater value than the male counterpart.

3.10.3 THE EMPLOYER'S DEFENCE
Apart from where the employer can demonstrate that the woman's work is not 'like work' or work of 'equal value' which relies on differences of practical importance, the law provides a defence where there exists a 'material difference' between the man's job and that of the woman which is not the difference of sex.

Material differences are regarded as those which are concerned with who does the work rather than relating to what work is done. The work might be like work, work rated as equivalent or work of equal or greater value but nonetheless the employer is afforded a defence if there exists a material difference in respect of who actually undertakes the work. The difference must be significant and relevant and may well go beyond what an individual brings to any job in question in terms of skill, experience, training or productivity.

An example of a material difference would be where a man doing similar work to a woman is paid more because of a sales related bonus that was available to both or because he happens to have been employed longer by the employer and it is their business policy to reward long service.

3.10.4 REMEDY

Any employee wishing to bring an equal pay claim may do so upon application to an employment tribunal at any time during employment or within 6 months of the effective date of termination of employment. The tribunal may make a declaration as to the inequality and is, as a result of recent case law, empowered to award up to 6 years arrears of pay up to the point where proceedings were commenced.

The Equal Opportunities Commission (see Useful Addresses) can provide invaluable advice to anyone contemplating an equal pay action, in particular as to the prospects of a successful claim given the particular facts and circumstances. As this section has indicated, such claims are notoriously complex for the unassisted litigant.

3.11 CASE STUDY

Kevin stacks shelves in Martin's '8' till late' food emporium. Kevin has three months' service and, under a contract of employment reluctantly given to him by Martin, is entitled to one month's notice of termination.

Martin, in a wild mood swing, dismisses Kevin one Monday morning telling him to collect his things and go home out of his sight.

Kevin seeks legal advice and is told, firstly, he has no right to demand to work his notice. Secondly, because Kevin was ready, willing and able to work his notice but was not requested to do so, Martin must pay him one month's money in lieu of working his notice. Martin can pay the notice in lieu in one of two ways. He can pay Kevin weekly in the normal manner, until the expiry of one month, and if he does the contract will continue for one month and Kevin will be on 'garden leave'. Alternatively, Martin can bring the contract to an immediate end, pay Kevin one month's money up front, in lieu of notice.

In addition, Kevin is told that if the contract continues for a further month he will be entitled to any other benefits that may run for the month. For example, an employer's pension contribution or accrued holiday entitlement. Likewise, if the contract is brought to an immediate end, he is told that he should receive compensation for loss of the benefits that he would have received had he been allowed to work out his notice period.

CHAPTER FOUR
UNFAIR DISMISSAL

4.1 THE PRINCIPLE
The law provides protection for an employee from being unfairly dismissed from their job or from being forced out of their work by the actions of their employer. To claim unfair dismissal the employer must have clearly terminated the contract of employment orally, in writing or by their conduct. Where there has been no dismissal but the employer has acted so unreasonably as to force the employee to resign their position, this is known as 'constructive dismissal' and the employee may act as if dismissed by the employer. It should be noted that the law will only recognise an employee's right to claim constructive dismissal where it can be shown that the employer has acted in serious breach of contract. A minor breach will not be enough to warrant resignation and a constructive dismissal claim.

Examples of serious breaches would include imposing, against the employee's wishes, changes to hours, pay, work location and the nature of the task to be performed or being in serious breach of the implied term of mutual trust and confidence. In most cases an employment tribunal hearing a constructive dismissal claim would have expected the employee to have first exhausted all internal avenues of grievance with the employer and not to have resigned as a first option. Constructive dismissal is largely a last resort action requiring fundamental or serious breach of contract by the employer. 'Resign or be sacked' situations resulting in a resignation would also be covered by an application to an employment tribunal for constructive dismissal.

Finally, it should be noted that the non-renewal of a fixed term contract by the employer is a dismissal and therefore can amount to an unfair dismissal. It is no longer possible for employees employed under fixed term contracts to agree to waive their unfair dismissal rights.

4.2 THE EXCLUSIONS
Not all employees are protected from being unfairly dismissed. The following conditions apply:

- The employee must have been employed for at least 1 year's continuous service.
- The employee, male or female, must not at the time of dismissal (or resignation) be over their normal retirement age for that employer, or where none exists, over 65 years old.
- The provisions do not apply to share fishermen.
- Those employed in the police service.

- In certain situations employees dismissed in connection with a lock-out or strike, are prevented from claiming protection against unfair dismissal. (An employee is protected for the first 8 weeks of participation in official industrial action or if the employer has failed to take reasonable procedural steps to resolve the dispute).

If the employee is excluded by reason of one of the above, they will not be able to challenge the unfairness or unreasonableness of their employer's actions whatever the circumstances. Their only hope of redress will be a claim for breach of contract (sometimes confusingly called "wrongful dismissal") against the employer. Such matters are dealt with in detail later.

4.3 THE EMPLOYER'S DEFENCE

The employee must first prove that they have, in fact, been dismissed or constructively dismissed. Once this is done and in most cases this is straightforward, the employer is then under a legal obligation, if challenged by the employee, to show that the dismissal was for one of 5 permitted potentially fair reasons for dismissal. It follows that these reasons may afford the employer a defence to their act of dismissal. They are:

1. Capability or qualifications;
2. The employee's conduct;
3. Redundancy;
4. Statutory requirements;
5. Some other substantial reason.

These categories require further explanation.

4.3.1 CAPABILITY AND QUALIFICATIONS

Generally "capability" will include the following elements:

- The employee's skill in the performance of their duties.
- The aptitude of the employee concerned in relation to the job for which they are employed.
- Their physical and mental ability to perform the tasks required.

"Qualifications", on the other hand, is described as any degree, diploma or other academic, technical or professional qualification relevant to that person's position as an employee. The absence of capability or qualification need only exist in relation to a significant part of their job. The employer need not show that all the tasks an employee is requested to undertake are affected by the lack of these two factors.

4.3.2 CONDUCT

Or, more to the point misconduct, is for obvious reasons a potentially fair reason for dismissal. The law supplies no definition of "conduct". However, it does include acts of gross misconduct, for example:

- Theft.
- Fraud.
- Violence.
- Damage to the employer's property.
- An act of dishonesty.
- Sexual harassment.
- Inciting racial tension or hatred.
- A significant act of negligence.
- Alcohol abuse at work.
- Insubordination, etc.

(This list is not exhaustive).

Conduct will also include acts of ordinary misconduct such as;

- Persistent poor time-keeping.
- Persistent absenteeism.
- Attitude problems.
- Carelessness, etc.

(This list is not exhaustive).

An act of gross misconduct and one of ordinary misconduct are, as the lists show, quite different in nature. Gross misconduct is so serious that it acts to bring the contract of employment to an immediate end without warning or notice to the employee provided always that they have had an opportunity to defend their position against the initial allegation before the employer arrives at their decision. An act of gross misconduct will therefore provide an employer with a potentially fair reason for dismissal. Ordinary misconduct does not bring the contract to an immediate end. In order for the employer to have a defence against dismissal for such conduct they must usually have followed a fair disciplinary procedure in respect of warnings. In practice, tribunals require the application of the ACAS Code of Practice on Disciplinary Practice and Procedures which requires the implementation of four stages:

1. A verbal warning;
2. A first written warning;
3. A final written warning;
4. Dismissal.

There should be an opportunity for the employee to state their case prior to the imposition of each stage of the procedure. Failure to follow a similar procedure may take away the employer's defence of a potentially fair reason for dismissal. These matters are dealt with in more detail in Chapter 7.

4.3.3 REDUNDANCY

It is a potentially fair reason for dismissal where an employee's contract of employment has been terminated because their job has diminished considerably or ceased to exist at their normal place of work. In short, because they are no longer required by the business and are redundant. Chapter 6 of this book is devoted exclusively to this area of employment law and the rights available to employees faced with this situation.

4.3.4 STATUTORY REQUIREMENTS

This potentially fair reason for dismissal is aimed at those situations where an employer has to dismiss an employee because they are not able to continue in that job without contravening some law. For example, a van driver who loses their driving licence because of a drink driving conviction, for 12 months, will not be able to undertake driving duties for their employer during that period of time without being in contravention of Road Traffic Law which requires a valid driving licence.

4.3.5 SOME OTHER SUBSTANTIAL REASON

This fifth potentially fair reason was designed to be a 'catch-all' for those reasons that did not fall neatly into the other 4 categories but nonetheless should rightfully, on their facts, provide the employer with a defendable position in law. Over the years one common type of dismissal persistently presents itself within this group. That is, where an employer re-organises their business and as a necessary part of that restructuring is forced to impose contract changes on the employee. The business re-organisation falling short of a full blown redundancy but similarly being driven by economic factors. In such situations to dismiss an employee who refuses to accept such contract changes will be a potentially fair dismissal 'for some other substantial reason'.

4.4 AUTOMATIC UNFAIR DISMISSALS

Having dealt with those situations which are potentially fair and which allow the employer a defence, there are a number of types of dismissal which if proven on their facts, fit within those categories of dismissal deemed "automatically unfair" and will not allow the employer any defence at all.

Those sub-sections below marked by an asterisk "*" have no one-year service requirement and employees over the normal retiring age or over the age of 65 are not barred from pursuing a complaint.

4.4.1 TRADE UNION MEMBERSHIP *

It is automatically unfair to dismiss an employee because they were, or proposed to become, a member of an independent trade union.

4.4.2 TRADE UNION ACTIVITY *

Where an employee is dismissed for having taken, or having proposed to take part in the activities of an independent trade union, outside working hours or within working hours if permitted by the employer, they will be deemed to have been automatically unfairly dismissed.

4.4.3 CLOSED-SHOP DISMISSALS *
It is automatically unfair to dismiss an employee for refusing to become or to remain a member of an independent trade union.

4.4.4 ASSERTION OF A STATUTORY RIGHT *
Where an employee seeks to assert a statutory right (for example to demand a written statement of particulars of employment) and is dismissed, that employee will be deemed to have been automatically unfairly dismissed. The reason behind this law is to prevent employers from victimising employees by fear of dismissal if all they seek is the enforcement or application of their statutory rights.

4.4.5 PREGNANT EMPLOYEES *
To dismiss an employee solely because she is pregnant or for any reason predominantly connected with her pregnancy or on grounds related to childbirth or maternity leave will be regarded in law as an automatically unfair dismissal. Employees also have the right not to be subjected to any detriment or victimised for reasons related to pregnancy, childbirth or maternity.

4.4.6 HEALTH AND SAFETY – RELATED DISMISSALS *
Employees are protected from dismissal where they:

- Carry out health and safety activities on behalf of their employer.
- Bring to the attention of the employer a concern over a risk to health and safety.
- Propose to leave, or leave the work place and refuse to return while danger persists, in the event that they reasonably believe their well-being is in serious and imminent danger and which cannot reasonably be averted.
- In the circumstances immediately above, take appropriate steps to protect themselves or others from danger.

There is no maximum compensatory award.

4.4.7 SHOPWORKERS AND SUNDAY TRADING *
From August 1994 the law has recognised types of shop worker in respect of Sunday trading:

- The protected shop worker.
- The opted-in shop worker.
- The opted-out shop worker.

In brief, the protected shop worker is one who before that date was not employed to work Sundays. Where the employee is asked to work Sundays and has no objection, by written notice to the employer the employee thereby becomes "opted-in" and no longer a "protected shop worker". The employee is under no legal obligation to comply with the employers request in such circumstances. The employee has freedom of choice. The notice to the employer must be:

- Written.
- Signed.
- Dated.
- Clearly state that there is no objection to working Sundays.

An "opted-out" worker is one who is not protected but, in complying with similar formalities above, has given their employer clear notice of their objection to Sunday working. To prevent the disturbance to the employer that may ensue if employees were allowed to opt-in and out with alarming regularity, the employer may insist that for a period of 3 months after having received an opting-out notice the employee undertakes Sunday work.

Every new employee has the right to receive from the employer an explanatory statement that they may choose to work or not to work on Sundays. If the employee wishes to object to Sunday work and does so within the first 8 weeks of service the employer is discharged from the obligation to provide an explanatory statement. In these circumstances workers who object will become "opted-out" shopworkers. The right to work or not to work on Sundays as a shopworker applies irrespective of length of service.

It is automatically unfair to dismiss a shopworker for refusing to work on a Sunday where they are either protected or opted-out.

4.4.8 OFFICIAL INDUSTRIAL ACTION AND DISMISSAL *

The dismissal of an employee for participating in official industrial action will be automatically unfair if it occurs during the first 8 weeks of such participation. A dismissal will also be unfair after that period if the employer has failed to take reasonable procedural steps to resolve the dispute. Unfairly dismissed strikers will be entitled to reinstatement only after a strike is over.

There is no equivalent protection for employees participating in unofficial industrial action.

4.4.9 UNOFFICIAL INDUSTRIAL ACTION AND DISMISSAL

The major difference between dismissals in the event of unofficial and official industrial action is that, where unofficial, the employer is given greater latitude by the law in being permitted to selectively dismiss and re-engage without penalty. This, in practice, will allow an employer to dismiss the perceived 'ring-leaders' of the industrial action. Industrial action will not be considered unofficial where:

- The employee is a trade union member and the action is authorised or endorsed by the union.
- The employee is not a trade union member but trade union members are taking part in the action and it has been authorised or endorsed by that union.

However, industrial action will not be regarded as unofficial if none of those participating are members of the trade union.

Industrial action may become unofficial if repudiated by the trade union. It will be classed unofficial with effect from the working day that immediately follows the date of repudiation.

4.4.10 PRESSURE DISMISSALS *

An employer who dismisses an employee because of pressure from a trade union, by way of the threat of industrial action, will be dismissing that employee unfairly.

4.4.11 DISMISSALS ON A TRANSFER OF AN UNDERTAKING

Transfers of undertakings or business transfers are dealt with in detail in Chapter 11. However, it should be noted in this section of the book that to dismiss an employee "further to" a business transfer will be regarded as, on the face of it, unfair. The dismissal may be before or after the transfer and the employer is only afforded a defence if they can show that the reason for dismissal was either an economic, technical or organisational reason that would necessarily lead to changes being required in the workforce.

4.4.12 DISMISSAL AND THE NATIONAL MINIMUM WAGE *

It is automatically unfair to dismiss a worker simply because the employer does not wish to pay the National Minimum Wage or because the employee has taken action to enforce their rights to the NMW. In addition if a worker is 'subjected to any detriment', such as hours being reduced, they may bring a claim in the employment tribunal from the first day of employment.

4.4.13 DISMISSAL FOR PUBLIC INTEREST DISCLOSURE *

The Public Interest Disclosure Act 1998 protects employees who 'blow the whistle' about wrongdoing. In certain circumstances, disclosures are protected and the employees who make them similarly protected. Employees are protected from unfair dismissal and from suffering any other detriment from their employer. Detriment may take a number of forms, such as denial of promotion, facilities or training opportunities that the employer would have otherwise offered.

Certain kinds of disclosure qualify for protection, for example, where the employee reasonably believes one or more of the following matters are either happening, took place in the past, or are likely to happen in the future:

* A criminal offence;
* The breach of a legal obligation;
* A miscarriage of justice;
* A danger to the health and safety of any individual;
* Damage to the environment; or
* Deliberate covering up of information tending to show any of the above five matters.

The reasonable belief held by the employee might be discovered subsequently to be, in fact, wrong. This will not matter provided it was a reasonably held belief in the circumstances at the time of disclosure. The employee may make the disclosure to the employer or a third party if they reasonably believed they would be subject to a detriment by the employer if disclosure were made to them.

Employees protected by the provisions who have been dismissed or have suffered other detriment can complain to an employment tribunal. The complaint should be made within three months of the dismissal or detriment. For unfair dismissal claims, interim relief is also available, provided the claim is made within seven days of the effective date of termination of employment. There is no limit to the amount of compensation that may be claimed.

4.4.14 WORKING TIME CASES *

It is automatically unfair to dismiss an employee for refusing to forgo a right conferred on him by the Working Time Regulations 1998 (e.g. the right to 4 weeks' paid annual leave) or refusing to comply with a requirement imposed on him by the employer in contravention of those Regulations (e.g. refusing to work on average over 48 hours per week). In addition, it is also unlawful to subject an employee to a detriment for reasons related to the Regulations.

4.4.15 PENSION SCHEME TRUSTEES *

An employee's dismissal is automatically unfair if the reason relates to the employee performing his functions as a trustee of a pension scheme related to his employment.

4.4.16 TRADE UNION RECOGNITION *

It is automatically unfair to dismiss an employee on grounds related to compulsory trade union recognition or de-recognition and it is unlawful to take adverse action short of dismissal on these grounds.

4.4.17 DISMISSAL FOR EXERCISING RIGHT OF ACCOMPANIMENT AT DISCIPLINARY HEARINGS *

An employer who dismisses an employee for exercising his statutory right to be accompanied at a disciplinary hearing, or for accompanying another employee, will be dismissing that employee unfairly. An employee also has the right not to be subjected to any detriment on these grounds.

4.4.18 PARENTAL LEAVE DISMISSALS *

The dismissal of an employee for taking parental leave is automatically unfair and it is unlawful to victimise him for reasons relating to parental leave.

4.4.19 TIME OFF FOR FAMILY EMERGENCIES DISMISSALS *

If the reason for dismissal relates to the employee exercising his right to time off to deal with family emergencies, this is automatically unfair. In addition, it is also unlawful to subject an employee to a detriment for reasons relating to time off for family emergencies.

4.4.20 EMPLOYEE REPRESENTATIVES *
An employee's dismissal will automatically be regarded as unfair if the reason relates to the employee carrying out his functions as an employee representative (or a candidate for election as such a representative) on a transfer of an undertaking or where the employer proposes to make collective redundancies.

4.4.21 REDUNDANCY *
To be selected for dismissal on the ground of redundancy for any of the reasons stated above (other than that in section 4.4.11).

4.5 THE FAIRNESS OF DISMISSAL
No analysis of unfair dismissal would be complete without there being some attempt to understand how the courts view a fair dismissal within the 5 categories of potentially fair dismissals (see section 4.3). It is the role of an employment tribunal to consider all the facts of a particular case and to determine whether in all the circumstances the dismissal was fair and reasonable. The employer having dismissed an employee will be under an initial burden to defend their action and base it within one of the 5 potentially fair reasons for dismissal. Having done that, the tribunal will then look into the following factors:

- Was the reason for dismissal sufficient given the facts of the case?
- What are the size and administrative resources available to the employer?
- Was there sufficient investigation by the employer prior to the decision to dismiss?
- Was there a fair hearing for the employee prior to the decision to dismiss?

Having looked at these elements, the tribunal must then ask itself whether, in accordance with equity and the substantial merits of the case, it believes the employer acted reasonably in dismissing the employee.

Any employee seeking to assert their rights in respect of unfair dismissal should understand in advance how the tribunal will regard the facts of the case. One aspect of procedural fairness does appear certain. That is, the employee's right to be heard before the decision to dismiss or not is made by the employer. This matter is dealt with in more detail in Chapter 7 but in summary the principle is this. No employee should be dismissed without first being given an opportunity to state their case, however obvious the misconduct or need for redundancy etc. may seem. Failure to allow the employee this right will be regarded as an unfair dismissal on procedural grounds alone.

4.6 FAIRNESS AND THE FIVE POTENTIALLY FAIR REASONS FOR DISMISSAL

4.6.1 CAPABILITY AND QUALIFICATIONS

For an employer to dismiss an employee on the grounds that they were incapable of performing the tasks required of them the employer must satisfy the tribunal that they honestly felt this to be the case. In exceptional cases the employer may come to this decision without following any formal procedure with the employee concerned. For example, when it can be demonstrated that the employee clearly knew what was expected of them and were equally clearly incapable of reaching that standard of work or of improving to reach that standard in the foreseeable future. In most cases, before such a conclusion may be drawn, the employer must adopt a fair procedure. Such a procedure would be expected to include the following:

- Monitoring of the employee.
- Face to face meetings with the employee to discuss the problem openly.
- Clear details of the employee's shortcomings.
- Implementation of a fair warnings procedure (see Chapter 7) if the employee fails to improve their performance.
- Reasonable opportunity to improve.
- Careful consideration of training requirements by the employer.
- Consideration of alternative work for which the employee may be more suited.

Dismissal of an employee for not having the required qualifications is rare, since most of the relevant information should have been checked by the employer at interview stage or shortly thereafter. If an employee misleads an employer at interview or within the job application in respect of qualifications and the employer subsequently discovers the truth, the employee may reasonably be dismissed if the required qualifications are essential for the performance of the job. Also, the dismissal may be without notice for gross misconduct because of the dishonesty involved on the part of the employee. If, however, during the course of employment a qualification is taken away (e.g. loss of driving licence) the employee should only be dismissed if it is not reasonable or possible to provide suitable employment in some other capacity. Employees who are offered another job by the employer in those circumstances must be prepared to change their contract of employment accordingly, possibly to the extent of accepting less pay if the job is of a lower grade.

An employee may become incapable of working due to ill-health. Before dismissing an employee who is ill the employer is obliged to consider any medical evidence reasonably available. Often this will necessitate requesting the permission of the employee to approach their doctor or consultant for a report. The employee may refuse permission, but if they do, the employer will be able to make a decision on their future employment without the benefit of an expert medical opinion. This decision may not favour the employee. Having obtained a report from the employee's doctor, the employer is in a position to make a reasoned decision as to the employee's future employment with their business. The employer must consider:

- The needs of the business.
- The prospects of a quick return to work by the employee.
- The availability of lighter duties to help the employee in getting back to work.
- The employee's past record of health.
- The nature of the illness and the likelihood of illness recurring.
- The likelihood of a full recovery and return to full duties.
- Finally, the employer should consult the employee before taking any decision to dismiss them.

Failure to follow a procedure such as that above may well be viewed by the tribunal as an unfair dismissal.

4.6.2 CONDUCT

Many of the procedural requirements which make dismissal for misconduct potentially fair are dealt with in Chapter 7. It is sufficient at this stage to outline the requirements. Other than in cases of gross misconduct, a dismissal for misconduct must have been subject to the following:

- Proper investigation of the facts by the employer. (This applies equally to gross misconduct).
- Implementation of a fair warnings procedure.
- A fair hearing of the employee's case at each stage of the warnings procedure.
- The implementation of a reasonable disciplinary sanction at each stage of the warnings procedure.
- That credit is given to the employee in respect of 'old' warnings that may reasonably be deemed to have lapsed by passage of time (usually 12 months or more).
- Consistent treatment with similar misconduct.

In the case of an allegation of gross misconduct, the employer is still required to convene a disciplinary hearing. If at that hearing the employer has an honest belief, based on reasonable grounds after all reasonable investigation, that the employee did act as alleged, there may be a finding of dismissal without notice on the ground of gross misconduct.

4.6.3 REDUNDANCY

Redundancy is dealt with in detail in Chapter 6 since, in its own right, it has proven to be a hotbed of dispute and litigation over the years.

What may be emphasised at this stage is that for a dismissal on the ground of redundancy to be potentially fair there must be:

- Prior meaningful consultation with any relevant employee.
- A fair selection of the employee(s) for redundancy.
- Full consideration of any alternative work available.
- Full consideration of any methods whereby redundancy may be avoided.
- A situation where the job at that place of work has diminished considerably or ceased to exist.

4.6.4 STATUTORY REQUIREMENTS

The mere fact an employer may be able to genuinely show, due to contravention of law, they are no longer able to employ a certain individual, this will not absolve them from the responsibility of following a fair procedure in implementing that dismissal. The procedure should include:

- A full consultation with the employee concerned.
- Full exploration (if appropriate) of suitable alternative employment with that business.

4.6.5 SOME OTHER SUBSTANTIAL REASON

As previously stated, two main types of dismissal which habitually fall into this category are those involving a business re-organisation and changes to the employee's contract of employment. In each of these cases and in all the others within this category of dismissals, formal procedures on consultation and hearings are pre-requisites before the dismissal will be regarded as potentially fair. Whatever the pressing business needs of the employer, the tribunal will invariably not accept that any commercial situation is so urgent that employees may be unfairly treated in substance or by the failure to observe procedural fairness and ordinary principles of natural justice.

4.7 WRITTEN REASONS FOR DISMISSAL

Every employee who has at least 1 year's continuous service with their employer and who is dismissed, is entitled to request a written statement of reasons for that dismissal from the employer. The employee may make their request orally or in writing and the employer must comply with the request within 14 days. In addition, an employee who is dismissed during pregnancy or maternity leave, irrespective of length of service, is entitled to a written statement of reasons for dismissal without having to request it. In practice it is well worth making the request and many employers make the mistake of supplying reasons which in fact only lend support to a claim for unfair dismissal. The written statement is admissible in evidence in any tribunal proceedings.

Should the employer refuse the request, on that point alone, the employee may bring a complaint before an employment tribunal.

Application may also be made where the reasons supplied are inadequate or untrue. The claim must be presented within 3 months from the effective date of termination of employment.

If well-founded, the complaint may lead to an award against the employer to pay the employee a sum equal to 2 weeks' pay and a declaration as to what the real reasons were for the termination.

4.8 UNFAIR DISMISSAL – THE REMEDIES

When an employee has succeeded in their claim for unfair dismissal and persuaded a tribunal to make a finding in their favour, they are entitled to choose whether they wish to return to the job or compensation. Returning to work is known as reinstatement or re-engagement.

The difference between the two is that reinstatement provides return to the same job whilst re-engagement is the return to a comparable job if this is practicable.

4.8.1 REINSTATEMENT

This is an order made by the tribunal that the employer shall treat the complainant (ex-employee) in all respects as if they had not been dismissed. The tribunal will consider:

- The wishes of the complainant.
- Whether it is practicable for an employer to comply with such an order if it were made.
- The conduct of the complainant when they were employed in so far as whether it would be just to make an order for reinstatement.

In practice, the employer is entitled to object to an order being made and the tribunal will consider evidence from the employer in respect of the following:

- Whether further conflict or industrial unrest would follow.
- The resources of the employer.
- Whether it would lead to a redundancy situation if the complainant had already been replaced.
- Whether it would result in over-manning.

If the employer's argument against reinstatement fails, the tribunal will clarify for the employer and complainant:

- Arrears of pay.
- Other financial benefits payable.
- The rights which must be restored to the complainant upon returning to work.
- The date by which the employer must comply with the order.

4.8.2 RE-ENGAGEMENT

This order is one in which the employer is told to engage the complainant in a comparable position to that from which they were originally dismissed. If in the time between dismissal and the tribunal decision, the original business has been taken over by another, the tribunal has the power to order the successor to re-engage the complainant. The tribunal will hear objections to the order and take into account the points raised in section 4.8.1 above. Particular to a re-engagement order the tribunal will clarify:

- The employer (in the event of a take-over situation).
- The type of employment.
- The wage or salary to be paid.
- Arrears of pay.
- Other financial benefits.
- Rights to be restored to the complainant upon return to work.
- The date by which the employer must comply with the order.

4.8.3 GENERALLY

It should be noted that whilst a tribunal will consider the changed circumstances of the employer post-dismissal, it will not allow the mere fact that the employee has been replaced to provide a defence for the employer. That would make the avoidance of reinstatement and re-engagement orders too easy. The employer must show that to replace was necessary or that a temporary replacement pending the case at employment tribunal was not practicable in the circumstances.

4.8.4 THE EMPLOYER REFUSES TO REINSTATE OR RE-ENGAGE

This is the situation where a tribunal orders reinstatement or re-engagement but, for whatever reason, the employer flatly refuses to comply with the order. In such circumstances the tribunal is empowered to make what is known as an additional award. This is an amount of compensation of between 26 and 52 weeks' pay up to a maximum of £230 per week.

The maximum amount is therefore: 52 x £230 = £11,960. The additional award is made (as it implies) on top of other awards, typically the basic and compensatory awards.

4.8.5 THE BASIC AWARD

Where it is impractical to order reinstatement or re-engagement, the employee must look to financial compensation. The first element of compensation will be the basic award which is payable when there is a finding of unfair dismissal. The amount to which the employee is entitled is dependent upon the following:

- The age of the employee.
- Their length of service.
- Their average gross weekly wage.

Calculation is made by taking into account a maximum sum of £230 per week and a maximum length of service of 20 years starting at the end of the period of service and working backwards in complete years. The employee is entitled to;

- 1½ weeks' pay for each year during which the employee was aged 41-64 inclusive.
- 1 weeks' pay for each year during which the employee was aged 22-40 inclusive.
- ½ weeks' pay for each year during which the employee was less than 22 years of age.

The maximum basic award is: 20 x 1.5 x £230=£6,900

In the event that the effective date of dismissal falls after the employee's 64th birthday the basic award will be reduced by one-twelfth for each complete month by which their age exceeds 64 years.

The amount of the basic award may be further reduced in the following circumstances:

- Where the conduct of the complainant prior to dismissal would make it just and equitable to do so.
- Where the complainant has unreasonably refused an offer made by the employer which would have had the effect of reinstatement prior to the tribunal hearing.
- Where the complainant has already received from their employer an ex-gratia payment of such an amount that it may be seen as sufficient to cover the amount of any basic award.
- Where a redundancy payment has been awarded by the tribunal or paid by the employer, by the amount of that payment (provided the employee was redundant).

4.8.6 EXCEPTION

The amount of the basic award will be 2 x £230 (two weeks' pay) where the reason for the dismissal was redundancy and the employee:

- Unreasonably refused or left suitable alternative employment.
- Was re-engaged or reinstated by the employer and there was, in effect, no dismissal.

4.8.7 COMPENSATORY AWARD

The amount the tribunal may grant as a compensatory award may be anything up to a maximum statutory ceiling figure of £50,000. (This amount is altered annually). In deciding how much it should award, a tribunal will take into account several factors. The loss to the complainant, including:

- Expenses reasonably incurred as a result of the dismissal.
- Loss of employment rights.

Other damages are assessed in accordance with their net value and include:

- Loss of wages, from the effective date of termination to the hearing.
- Future loss of earnings.
- Loss of personal use of a company car.
- Loss of benefits in kind. For example, medical insurance, free accommodation, free roadside assistance membership, contribution or payment of telephone bills, loss of use of mobile phone or lap-top computer etc.
- Pension rights. Particularly in respect of final salary schemes.
- Loss of statutory rights. This covers the loss of employment protection for the first year of service, statutory redundancy pay and the entitlement to statutory minimum notice.

Awards are commonly in the region of £200 for loss of statutory rights. As with the basic award, the compensatory award may be reduced by the tribunal. Factors taken into account include:

- Contributory fault on the part of the complainant whilst in employment. The tribunal is at liberty to reduce the amount by 100%.
- Did the unfairness of the dismissal make any difference?
- Mitigation.
- Payments already made by the employer.

In respect of whether or not the unfairness of the dismissal made any difference, this is recently of less importance to the tribunal than it had been for some years. Tribunals will look not at whether the failure to adopt a fair procedure made any difference to the decision, but what would have happened if a fair procedure had been adopted. For example, it may be provable by the employer that even if a fair procedure had been implemented, due to economic necessity, several weeks later a genuine redundancy would have been imposed on the employee in question.

Mitigation of loss is evident in all areas of law and employment is no exception. In essence, it is an obligation on the employee, having been dismissed, to do everything reasonably practicable to secure alternative work. In short, employees will be penalised by the tribunal if in its opinion they have not made reasonable attempts to obtain some suitable alternative work. The burden of proving that the complainant has not made every effort to reasonably mitigate their loss is on the employer. Should the complainant incur necessary expenditure in attempting to mitigate their loss (e.g. travel etc.) such amounts are recoverable within the compensatory award.

As with the basic award, any amounts paid to the complainant by their former employer will be taken into account in the assessment of the compensatory award. There may be cases where the complainant received state benefits from the date of dismissal. Where this occurs the tribunal must identify how much of the award covers lost earnings. This amount may then have deducted from it the state benefit element which may be recouped by the State. The order of deductions is as follows:

- Calculate the total loss suffered by the employee.
- Deduct any payments made by the former employer.
- Make any reduction for whether the fairness of the dismissal made any difference and make any reduction for failure to mitigate loss.
- Make any reduction for contributory fault.
- Apply the statutory maximum.
- It is important to note that the statutory maximum is only applied after the reductions have been made.

4.8.8 ADDITIONAL AWARD – NON COMPLIANCE WITH AN ORDER

Where a tribunal orders reinstatement or re-engagement but it is not complied with by the employer an additional award may be made. The amount awarded will be not less than 26 or more than 52 weeks' pay. For the purposes of calculating an additional award a weeks' pay will not exceed £230. The maximum additional award is, therefore, £11,960.

4.8.9 INTEREST ON TRIBUNAL AWARDS

Interest will accrue on awards made by an industrial tribunal at the rate of 8% per annum starting 42 days after the tribunals decision is despatched to the parties in the case. Interest is simple not compound and accrues on a daily basis. Awards of costs or expenses do not carry interest.

4.9 SETTLEMENT

There are two forms of settlement acceptable in law.

4.9.1 ACAS SETTLEMENTS

Once proceedings have been issued before an employment tribunal, an ACAS officer in that region will automatically become involved with the case in an attempt to resolve the dispute by settlement through negotiation. Where agreement is achieved the details of the settlement are formalised in a document drafted by the ACAS officer known as a COT3 Settlement (so called after the form upon which it is written). COT3 Settlements are binding on both parties and are in effect full and final.

4.9.2 COMPROMISE AGREEMENTS

Where there is a dispute between employer and employee that could lead to proceedings being issued, in certain circumstances their differences may be settled using the compromise agreement facility. The document is usually (but not always) drafted by the employer's lawyer on the ground that they have more available resources than the employee. The compromise agreement is a simple means of resolving disputes but a number of conditions must be satisfied. For the agreement to be valid in law it must:

- Relate to a particular dispute between the parties.
- Be in writing.
- Have been agreed to by the employee, who must have received independent legal advice from either a qualified lawyer (solicitor or barrister not being the employer's lawyer) or a competent trade union officer or official or a competent advice centre worker.
- The independent adviser, as above, must be identified in the agreement.
- The independent adviser must be insured against claims for professional negligence.
- Contain a declaration that the formalities stated above are satisfied.

If the conditions are satisfied the agreement will be legally binding on both parties and will act as full and final settlement of the particular dispute.

4.10 CASE STUDY

Angela is a receptionist for Minster Insurance Limited. After only 6 weeks service she complains to Sally, her boss, that the equipment she is required to use is dangerous. It has a number of loose wires and when it gets hot, sparks can be seen, along with some smoke, coming out of the back of her telephone console.

Angela brings this matter to the attention of Sally time and time again but is ignored and told to stop 'whining' or she will be sacked. Angela honestly fears for her personal safety and raises the issue with Keith, Sally's superior.

Sally is incensed at Angela going behind her back and sacks her giving her a weeks' notice. Angela seeks legal advice.

Despite Angela's short length of service she is advised to claim unfair dismissal since she was sacked for bringing to the attention of her employer a serious health and safety concern which could have affected her or her colleagues. Her claim is successful and in addition the Health and Safety Executive prosecute Minster Insurance for having an unsafe place of work — they face a hefty fine.

CHAPTER FIVE

WRONGFUL DISMISSAL

5.1 THE DEFINITION

Wrongful dismissal should not be confused with unfair dismissal. The latter is a statutory right not to be dismissed unfairly. Wrongful dismissal derives from common law and is where the employee is not in breach of contract but where the employer decides to terminate the contract of employment by dismissing the employee without notice. The employer is then in breach of contract. The claim by the employee is for damages for breach of contract.

Until relatively recently, a wrongful dismissal claim could only be brought before a county court or High Court but it may now be brought as an action for breach of contract before an employment tribunal. The amount claimed by the employee will determine which court forum may be used. In some cases the employee will have a choice (see the table below).

AMOUNT IN DISPUTE	TYPE OF COURT
Less than £25,000	Employment tribunal or county court
Greater than £25,000	County court or High Court
(it may be given fast-track status subject to level of complexity)	

In order to bring such a claim the employee must be able to show that:

- They were dismissed in breach of contract and received no notice or less than the statutory minimum period of notice or less than the contractual notice, whichever is the greater; and
- They have suffered financially as a result of the employer's breach of contract.

Where the employee has a choice of court or tribunal in which to bring their action they should consider a number of advantages and disadvantages in the forum they choose. If an employee brings a wrongful dismissal claim in the county court or High Court they may invoke a number of useful procedural devices which are not available in employment tribunals.

5.2 THE COUNTY COURT AND HIGH COURT SUMMARY JUDGMENT

There is a procedure whereby an employee may apply for summary judgment in specific circumstances where the employee believes the employer has no real defence to the claim. The result can be very quick payment for the employee by order of the court or the employer being ordered to pay money into court as a condition of being granted leave to defend. This becomes a very useful tactic for the employee to exert pressure to pay on the reluctant employer. The court has the power to strike out a so-called defence of its own volition. Before filing the Allocation Questionnaire, the Claimant can simply write to the court asking the District Judge to determine whether the Defendant's reply should be treated as a defence. This is appropriate where the reply is an obvious play for time.

5.2.1 INTERIM PAYMENT

There is also a procedure whereby an employee may be able to seek an interim payment from the employer. This is possible where the employee has a strong case for payment and financial hardship will ensue if payment is unduly delayed. The three basic grounds on which an interim payment may be claimed are where:

1. The employer has admitted liability but contests the amount of damages.
2. The employee has obtained judgment against the employer for damages to be assessed.
3. If the action proceeded to trial, the employee would obtain judgment for substantial damages against the employer.

5.2.2 COUNTER-CLAIM

The county court, High Court and employment tribunals all have a procedure whereby the employer can put in a counter-claim. That is, the employer counter-claims that the employee owes them money for some reason. The circumstances in which an employer can bring a counter-claim are much more restricted in the employment tribunal system. This restriction may be to the advantage of the employee.

5.2.3 EMPLOYMENT TRIBUNALS

A wrongful dismissal claim of less than £25,000 before an employment tribunal also has some clear advantages. The two main ones being a quicker hearing of the case and that the employee is unlikely to have an award of costs made against them in the event they are unsuccessful. This latter point is significant since the other party's costs could run into thousands of pounds.

5.3 WAS THE EMPLOYEE DISMISSED?

There are several ways in which dismissal may be established.

5.3.1 DISMISSAL WITH NOTICE

This is the most straightforward and is where the employer terminates the contract of employment by giving the employee the required notice under the contract or by complying with the statutory minimum period of notice, whichever is the greater. It follows that any dismissal by the employer that fails to comply with either the contractual or statutory notice is a breach of contract and wrongful dismissal.

Where a contract of employment contains no provision for notice the court is entitled to impose what it determines is a reasonable period of notice. This may not be the statutory period of notice. For example, a salaried employee has been working for 6 months under a contract of employment. The contract says nothing about the provision of notice. The employee is paid regularly at monthly intervals. The employer terminates the contract and seeks to apply the statutory minimum period of notice by paying 1 week only. In this example it may be possible for the employee to bring an action for wrongful dismissal on the basis that by implication they are entitled to 1 month's notice by reference to their pay interval and their level of pay. The employee will be relying on the court to agree that on the facts, a reasonable period of notice would have been 1 month and no less.

This example is common in practice and in most cases the court would find in favour of the employee's claim if for no other reason than the employer should be penalised for failing to clarify the period of notice in the contract. Where the employee in question is particularly skilled, highly paid or in a position of seniority it is not inconceivable that the court would be prepared to imply a reasonable period of notice of 3 months to 1 year, should the contract be silent.

5.3.2 DISMISSAL WITHOUT NOTICE

Dismissal without notice may occur where the employee is allegedly guilty of:

- Gross misconduct.
- Gross negligence.
- Gross incompetence.

In all of these cases the termination of employment without notice which ensues will be a summary dismissal. Such immediate termination and the ability to implement such action on the part of the employer comes from common law. Put simply, it occurs when the employee has acted in such a way as to completely undermine the relationship of trust and confidence between them and the employer. The employee, by their act or omission, is often said to have 'smashed' the contract of employment rendering it inoperable from that point onwards. Another way in which such acts are commonly described is to say that the employee has acted in repudiatory (fundamental) breach of contract upon which the employer is entitled to respond by imposing summary dismissal.

However, not just any breach of contract by the employee will give rise to summary termination. The employer must always be able to justify the dismissal without notice. If the employer fails to prove a repudiatory breach on the part of the employee, the employee may regard themselves as having been wrongfully dismissed and therefore entitled to claim damages for breach of contract based upon the period of notice to which they are entitled under contract or statute.

In bringing an action for wrongful dismissal in such circumstances, the employee is in effect challenging the reason for summary dismissal. Any hearing must necessarily look at the alleged fault by the employee to determine whether the employer's response was justified. Depending on the facts of any particular case this may or may not be in the best interests of the employee.

To assist an employee in deciding whether to bring such an action following summary dismissal, it may be useful to consider the following:

- Had the employee acted in a similar way before during their employment?
- If yes, had the employer regarded the matter with such gravity?
- Had other employees similarly acted without being summarily dismissed?
- In all the circumstances, did the act or omission completely undermine the relationship of trust and confidence between the parties?

The first 3 points above are important, since the court or tribunal will look at the consistency of approach by the employer. If it does not exist, a finding of unjustified summary dismissal is likely.

5.3.3 THE EMPLOYEE RESIGNS

If the employer acts in such a way as to breach a fundamental term of the contract (for example, by failing to pay due wages or salary) they will be acting in repudiatory breach of the contract of employment. The employee then has a choice. They can continue with the contract and waive the right to take action for the repudiatory breach. Conversely, the employee may resign and sue the employer for breach of contract as if they had been dismissed.

5.4 THE EMPLOYEE IS NOT DISMISSED BUT RESIGNS IN BREACH OF CONTRACT

This is a common occurrence and it is therefore worth detailing at this juncture. Typically the situation is this. The employee is by contractual obligation under a legal duty to provide notice of their intended resignation from their position with the employer. This required notice may be 1 week, 1 month, 6 months or more, depending on the nature and wording of the contract. For one reason or another, usually because the employee has a better job offer to go to, the employee fails or refuses to give the employer the required period of notice under the contract. This failure is a breach of contract on the part of the employee. The employer may, in theory, bring an action for damages against the employee. The employer would have to bring their action before the High Court since they have no jurisdiction to issue proceedings against an employee in an employment tribunal.

In most cases it is not in the employer's best interests to sue the errant employee and quantifying loss before the court in such circumstances can be difficult. Certainly the employer cannot restrain the employee from leaving inside the notice period, since to allow such a legal remedy would be tantamount to slavery and unsupportable on the grounds of public policy. What then, if anything, can an employer do against the employee?

The answer is that only in a limited number of cases, with exceptional facts, will the courts be willing to prevent an employee from leaving an employer in breach of contract. Such cases would be where the employee is of significant importance to the employer, such as the editor of a national newspaper. Even then, no court order will demand that the employee works out the period of notice. Instead the employee is put on what is called 'garden leave'. That is, relieved of all duties and paid their salary at the normal interval for the duration of the notice period they should have given under the contract. In return, for that period they are restrained from taking-up employment elsewhere.

5.5 THE EMPLOYEE IS DISMISSED WITH PAY IN LIEU OF NOTICE

There are many occasions where the employee is dismissed by the employer and instead of being asked to work out the statutory or contractual period of notice they are paid 'in lieu' of notice. That is, receiving an equivalent sum of money to that which they would have earned had they worked out the period of notice. Where this occurs the general principle is that the employee will have no claim for wrongful dismissal. This is because the courts will view the payment in lieu as damages for wrongful dismissal, thus effectively taking away from the employee a right of action. It is important that the employee is put in the same financial position they would have been in if notice had been given. For example, if they have a company car for personal use, they should be compensated for loss of that car during what would have been the notice period (see section 5.10).

Two important aspects of this situation should be noted. Firstly, the employer has an absolute right to pay in lieu of notice whether or not this right is expressed in any way within the contract of employment. The second point is the logical reverse in that no employee has the right to demand to work their period of notice. The reason the courts adopt this approach is an unwillingness, for obvious reasons, to force an employer or employee to work for or with one another.

Since pay in lieu of notice is regarded as damages for breach of contract, impliedly, the employee should receive payment for the notice period net. That is, receive the same amount as they would have received had they worked that period. However, it is commonplace for employees to be paid in lieu of notice gross. Such amounts may, depending on the wording of the contract itself and the custom and practice of the employer, be liable to tax and National Insurance as earnings. Generally, there is great uncertainty as to the taxability of such payments and the employee should take as much care as the employer to ensure that liability is met or lawfully avoided. In any event, any damages are taxable to the extent that they exceed £30,000.

5.6 WRONGFUL DISMISSAL AND RESTRICTIVE COVENANTS

An employee may have within their contract of employment a number of restrictive covenants with which they must comply in the event of termination of the contract of employment. Examples would be:

- Not to work for a competitor of the employer within a specified period of time (usually 6 months to 1 year).
- Not to work for a competitor of the employer within a defined geographical area (usually linked to the time period above).
- Not to solicit clients of the employer for a specified period of time after termination of the contract.
- Not to entice away from the employer existing members of staff for a specified period of time after termination of the contract.

Other similar restraints may be agreed under contract. Chapter 13 deals with this issue in more detail. Should the employer wrongfully terminate the contract of employment, their ability to impose such conditions subsequently upon the employee may be in question. The principle applied by the courts is that a wrongdoer, in this case the employer, is not entitled thereafter to the support of the court in respect of other contract terms and conditions.

5.7 TIME LIMITS

Wrongful dismissal being a claim for breach of contract is subject to the normal contract claim limitation. All claims in the county court and High Court must be brought within 6 years of the breach of contract.

Recently, as indicated in section 5.1, the jurisdiction to hear breach of contract claims, including those for wrongful dismissal, has been extended to employment tribunals. They may now hear claims where the amount in dispute between the parties is less than £25,000. The employee must present his claim to the tribunal within 3 months from the effective date of termination. Where there is no such date, time will run from the last day upon which the employee worked in employment for that employer. Only in exceptional circumstances will the time limit of 3 months be extended. The courts will only extend if evidence is presented which shows that in all the circumstances of the case it was not reasonably practicable for the employee to present his claim in time. Breach of contract claims may only be made to an employment tribunal where the employee's employment has terminated. Existing employees must therefore make such a claim to the county or High Court.

5.8 SETTLING A CLAIM FOR WRONGFUL DISMISSAL

The employer may admit wrongful dismissal and wish to settle their dispute with the employee rather than go to court. In respect of an action that may be taken in the county court or High Court, the law provides that the parties can reach an agreement not to proceed to court provided the employee is in receipt of 'valuable consideration'. That is, some benefit (usually financial but not always) must be granted to the employee by the employer in return for the case being dropped. The complicating factor is the emergence of employment tribunals in respect of wrongful dismissal claims.

5.9 WRONGFUL DISMISSAL AND UNFAIR DISMISSAL – A SIMULTANEOUS ACTION

In theory, provided the employee is in no way excluded from bringing either action, they may bring claims for unfair dismissal and wrongful dismissal at the same time. This can now occur in two ways:

1. Both actions before an employment tribunal.
2. An action for unfair dismissal before a tribunal and/or additional action for wrongful dismissal before either the county court or High Court.

If both actions are before a tribunal the facts relating to each aspect of the claim will be heard at the same time and a decision will be made by the tribunal on each in a single judgment.

Where the wrongful dismissal claim is brought before the county court or High Court it is usual for the employer to request that the tribunal proceedings are stayed (put on hold) until the outcome of the wrongful dismissal action. Such a request will normally be granted. The reason for staying the tribunal action is because it is most commonly the least important financially of the two claims. It is a principle of law that the employee will not be entitled to recover twice for the same loss. Any award made in a tribunal may be taken into account by the county court or High Court and vice versa.

5.10 QUANTIFYING DAMAGES

Generally the employee is entitled to damages which equal the amount of wages or salary that they would have earned if the employer had not prematurely terminated the contract of employment. Additionally the employee may claim for any benefits in kind that would have been received during the notice period had it been worked.

The period of time over which these entitlements are assessed is from the point of wrongful termination to when the contract may have been lawfully terminated by the employer. In most cases this will be no more and no less than the period of notice that should have been given to the employee. In assessing the loss that is recoverable, the courts will consider two factors:

1. The employee must have been contractually entitled to the wage, salary or benefit in kind.
2. The period over which these amounts were due must be ascertainable. (In most cases the notice period is self-evident or the court will have little difficulty in implying a reasonable notice period over which to make the calculation).

5.10.1 WAGES AND SALARY

The amount of basic salary, whether expressly stated in the contract or included by implication, will be recoverable. The most common and reliable method of calculating the amount of basic salary over the period of notice is to assess the net salary over the relevant period. This sum should then be 'grossed-up'. The employee should then receive the amount remaining after tax and National Insurance liabilities have been deducted from the grossed-up sum. In many cases this will amount to the net sum payable over the period. Employees should be aware that taxation is likely to effect the amount of money received by order of the court. In addition, social security contributions received by the employee over the relevant period will be deducted from the amount recoverable.

5.10.2 ADDITIONAL AMOUNTS

An employee may customarily or under contract be in receipt of payments over and above that of basic salary. Such amounts include:

- Commission.
- Profit-related pay.
- Bonus entitlement.
- Gratuities (tips).

The amount recoverable is based on the employer denying the employee the opportunity of earning such payments. To evaluate this, the court will use:

- The wording of the contract.
- Oral agreement.
- Past performance.
- Custom and practice.

In looking at commission, profit-related pay and bonus payments the court will not necessarily assume that these would be payable in the amounts paid up until the date of dismissal. It may be possible for the employer to show that their business is poor post-dismissal and that would have affected the amounts payable under such provisions - the court will listen to this evidence. However, in most cases, the courts will look at past payments and apply an average amount payable over the relevant notice period.

Depending on the wording of the contract of employment, many bonus payments are discretionary by nature. If they are discretionary they will generally not be regarded as a contractual entitlement and are therefore not recoverable by the employee.

Holiday pay is another typical additional amount recoverable in wrongful dismissal actions. The amount payable will depend on the terms of the contract and any statutory entitlement. Generally a contract will state the annual entitlement, for example, 20 days. To calculate the entitlement the employee should divide the annual entitlement by 52 (representing the weeks in 1 year). This figure is then the rate of weekly accrual. This weekly figure should be multiplied by the number of weeks in the holiday year up to and including the date upon which the contract would have ended had due notice been issued. Finally any holiday taken in that holiday year should be deducted leaving the amount recoverable under the wrongful dismissal action. This amount is recoverable net only since it is a right derived under contract.

5.10.3 BENEFITS IN KIND
These will include:

- Company car.
- Accommodation.
- Pension Contributions.
- Medical Insurance.
- Interest free or low rate loans whilst in employment.

The basis of calculating all these amounts is the net value to the employee for the duration of the notice period.

5.10.4 OTHER LOSSES
Another possible element of damages is the loss of the opportunity to bring a successful claim for unfair dismissal. This may arise where, as a result of the wrongful dismissal, the one year period of qualifying service is not attained, but would have been had due contractual notice been given.

A claim for damages may also include an amount to compensate the employee as a result of the employer failing to follow a contractual disciplinary procedure. The employee will be able to claim damages for the time it would have taken the employer to go through the procedure (see section 7.11).

5.10.5 LOSSES NOT RECOVERABLE
Years ago the courts believed that damages for mental stress, anxiety, inconvenience, injured feelings and frustration could be claimed in an action for wrongful dismissal. With the advent of protection from

unfair dismissal in the employment tribunal system it is now felt that such matters are best entertained within that forum rather than under a breach of contract claim in the county court or High Court. The result is that such damages may not be awarded in a wrongful dismissal action. Compensation for the manner of dismissal has no place in damages awarded in wrongful dismissal actions. However, in very limited circumstances, damages for loss of reputation may be recoverable.

Perhaps the only other exception to this strict rule is that an apprentice under a contract of apprenticeship (usually two years) who is wrongfully dismissed, may recover a sum of damages to reflect the loss of future prospects, having been denied the opportunity of completing their apprenticeship contract. The amount will be based on the cost of re-training elsewhere.

5.11 MITIGATION

As discussed in Chapter 4 in relation to the compensatory award for unfair dismissal, the employee will be under a general duty to mitigate their loss. This includes actively looking for alternative employment and not unreasonably refusing such employment should the opportunity arise. The onus of proving that the employee has failed to mitigate their loss is on the employer. The duty to mitigate only begins once the contract has been breached by the employer – even where the employer has indicated in advance that they will dismiss the employee.

Moreover, the obligation to take reasonable alternative employment is more flexible towards the employee than at first it may appear. For example, just because an alternative job offers a similar wage or salary, this may not make it a suitable alternative position. The status and responsibility offered by the new position are matters the employee is entitled to take into account when making his decision to accept or reject the offer. On the other hand, to hold out for exactly the same salary, status and responsibility in difficult economic conditions may be regarded as a failure to make a reasonable effort to mitigate loss.

If a new position is secured, the employee will have mitigated their loss. This could be in full or in part. The new job may be lower paid. As a general rule the amount earned by the employee in their new job will be taken into account by the court and deducted from the total of the wrongful dismissal claim. The period between dismissal and new employment will remain recoverable, as will any shortfall in wage or salary between the old and new job for the duration of the notice period.

However, if the employer terminates the contract by making a payment in lieu of notice under an express clause of the contract which permits this, then the employer must pay the relevant amount in full, without any deduction for mitigation. This is because the employer has contractually promised the payment regardless of mitigation.

5.11.1 UNFAIR DISMISSAL COMPENSATION

Rarely is the basic award for unfair dismissal deducted from the damages awarded for wrongful dismissal. The compensatory award is a different matter. Amounts paid under a compensatory award may be deducted in so far as they correspond to heads of damages in the wrongful dismissal claim. This would mean that a certain proportion of the amount awarded for loss of earnings or additional payment at tribunal may reduce the value of the wrongful dismissal claim. In practice, this calculation which requires a defined composition of the compensatory award, is not simple. Suffice it to say in this context, that employees should be aware of a possible reduction to their damages as a result of this reasoning.

5.11.2 ACCELERATED RECEIPT

This is not applicable in the great majority of wrongful dismissal actions, for the simple reason that most people's entitlement to notice, whether contractual or statutory, is short. It may apply to those employees who are entitled to a period of notice of say 1 or 2 years, and the court makes its decision and awards damages before the expiry of the period of notice. In most cases the leaving date is some time after the expiry of the last day of notice had it been given.

Accelerated receipt is a mechanism used by the court to reduce an amount of damages awarded. It takes into account the possibility of occurrences that might affect employment until the end of the stated period of notice such as death, medical incapacity or the employee deciding to resign before the unexpired portion of the notice period. It also takes into account that the employee will be receiving a proportion of wages as damages, up front. Investment of these funds will in itself create some wealth that would not have been possible had the contract been worked by the employee. A normal rate of reduction is between 2 and 6 per cent.

5.11.3 INJUNCTIVE ACTION

There may be occasions when the employee is not satisfied with claiming damages for wrongful dismissal but wishes to restrain the employer from dismissing them. A possible remedy would be an application to the court for an injunction to restrain the employer from acting as they intend. The general rule is that injunctions for such matters are granted in only a few exceptional cases. The reason being the courts' reluctance to compel an employer to retain an employee since to do so may adversely affect commercial considerations and result in conflict between the two parties. As stated earlier in this chapter an injunction sought by the employer to restrain the employee from leaving inside the notice period is a similarly rare occurrence but for different reasons.

The exception to the general rule against granting an employee an injunction is where it can be manifestly proven that the relationship of trust and confidence between the parties is intact and that damages in themselves would be an inadequate remedy. In addition, the courts will give consideration to the size and resources of the employer. Large organisations and local authorities, for example, are more likely targets for a successful application for an injunction by an employee wrongfully dismissed. The test applied by the court to an injunction application is known as the 'balance of convenience'. The court will look at:

- The likelihood of success by the employee at full trial.
- The adequacy of damages as a remedy.
- Is there an issue of 'real significance' at stake?
- The impact of the injunction, if granted, on the employer's business.

To reiterate, in the vast majority of cases, the employee will stand little or no chance in persuading a court to grant an injunction restraining the employer from dismissing them wrongfully. Most claims are claims for damages for breach of contract only. Therefore, there can be little doubt that damages will be considered an adequate remedy.

5.12 CASE STUDY

Amanda works as a telesales operative for Keith Haddock Promotions Limited. She has 6 months' service. Keith can be a difficult boss and is particularly concerned about time keeping. Amanda arrives late for work for the third day in a row due to a delayed train service beyond her control. In a fit of temper Keith says, 'it's the last straw I'm sacking you with immediate effect for gross misconduct — collect your things and go!' Keith refuses to pay Amanda her 1 month's contractual notice. Amanda seeks legal advice.

Although the poor time keeping is deeply frustrating for Keith it is at worst ordinary misconduct for which Amanda should receive a verbal warning. The conduct is not serious enough to be gross misconduct warranting immediate termination of the contract. Amanda applies to an employment tribunal claiming wrongful dismissal. That is, a claim for money she should have received for the contractual period of notice (one month) and accrued holiday entitlement calculated up to the end of the notice period.

On the advice of his lawyers, Keith is forced to pay Amanda the total damages claimed since he has no proper defence to his hasty action. By issuing proceedings in the employment tribunal within 3 months of the date of dismissal, Amanda did not incur any issuing fees as would be the case in the county court.

CHAPTER SIX
REDUNDANCY

6.1 THE GENERAL SCHEME

In broad terms the statutory redundancy payment scheme entitles any employee with two years' service, who is dismissed for redundancy, a lump sum tax free, calculated according to age, length of service and gross weekly wage. This is the payment scheme. However, redundancy is more complex in practice. For a dismissal on that ground to be potentially fair it must genuinely exist. Furthermore, the employer, in terminating the contract of employment for that reason, must treat the employee fairly in the procedure they use prior to the final decision to dismiss. The redundancy must be provable on its facts and the employee must be fairly selected and then meaningfully consulted with a view to avoiding a redundancy if at all possible.

6.2 THE DEFINITION

The redundancy situation must exist on its facts. It must not be used as a convenient vehicle for removing an employee with whom the employer is, for some reason, disenchanted. The statutory definition provides that the dismissal must be attributable wholly or mainly to the fact that:

- The employer has ceased, or intends to cease, to carry on the business for the purposes for which the employee was employed by them, or has ceased, or intends to cease, to carry on that business in the place where the employee was employed; and/or
- The requirements of the business for the employee to carry out work of a particular kind in the place they were employed have ceased or diminished, or are expected to cease or diminish.

Typically there are three situations which give rise to a redundancy situation:

1. The employer closes their business or the part of their business in which the employee works.
2. Due to an economic downturn in demand the employee is no longer or will be no longer gainfully employed in their present position.
3. Due to a business reorganisation for economic and/or reasons of efficiency the employee's job has gone or been significantly reduced.

Most redundancy situations will fit one of the 3 categories above. When it does, the dismissal for redundancy which ensues will in all likelihood be potentially fair. It will only be made unfair if the employer fails to implement the decision procedurally correctly or fails to pay the employee what is rightfully due to them under contract or law. Employees should remember that where they suspect the redundancy situation is bogus, the burden of proving that a redundancy situation actually exists on its facts rests with the employer, if challenged.

6.2.1 AT THAT PLACE OF WORK

To be within the definition the redundancy situation must apply to the employee at their place of work. One problem which can occur is where the employee selected for redundancy is subject to a mobility clause within their contract of employment. That is, the contract has a term incorporated into it either expressly or impliedly (through custom and practice) that in the event of there being no work at one of the employer's sites, they may demand the employee moves to another where there is a plentiful supply of similar work.

The test for determining the place of work is primarily a factual one, although the employee's contractual terms may provide evidence of the place of work. Thus, if an employee has, as a matter of fact, worked in only one location, then the existence of a contractual mobility clause enabling the employer to move them to another site does not change the place of work. Therefore, the employer cannot avoid paying the statutory redundancy payment by relying on a mobility clause.

6.3 TIME OFF

Assuming the redundancy is fair and has been fairly implemented, any employee given notice of termination on the grounds of redundancy, is entitled to reasonable time off during the notice period to look for other work or make arrangements for necessary training. What is 'reasonable' is largely a matter of common sense and is deliberately not more precisely defined in law. The time off should be paid by the employer. The right is dependent upon the employee having 2 years' continuous service at the date upon which the dismissal notice is due to expire.

Most time off taken by employees is to attend interviews at the offices of prospective employers or with recruitment or employment agents. These appointments even if they amounted to 2 or 3 per week are likely to be regarded as reasonable if challenged by the employer. The employer has no right to demand proof of the appointments but it follows that to refuse to comply with a request may be seen as obstructive and could be unhelpful to the employee's claim that time off to attend such interviews is reasonable.

6.4 THE REDUNDANCY PAYMENT

Where a redundancy situation exists on its facts, the employee will be entitled to a redundancy payment. This entitlement remains whether or not the employee is fortunate enough to have secured alternative work with another employer. There are conditions to the payment:

- The individual must be an employee (not self-employed – see Chapter 1).
- The individual must have been employed for a continuous period with that employer of not less than 2 years.
- The employee must have been dismissed.
- The dismissal must be by reason of genuine redundancy.

6.4.1 CONTINUOUS EMPLOYMENT

Continuity of employment will be intact provided the employee (excluding periods of incapacity or holiday) does some work for the employer during any week in which they were under contract of employment. Put another way, any break in employment of more than 7 days to undertake work elsewhere, or to do no work at all by choice, may break continuity of service. Much depends on the facts of any particular case and what has been agreed between the parties. The transfer of ownership of a business from one employer to another will not break continuity and this occurrence is dealt with in Chapter 11. The relevant date for the purpose of calculating the continuous period of 2 years will be:

- Where the employee is given notice, the date upon which that notice expires.
- Where no notice is given, the date upon which termination takes effect.

Where the employee is paid in lieu of notice either:

- The last day of work, where the notice is paid in a lump sum.
- The date on which notice expires where the employee receives normal payments but is relieved of all duties for the duration of the notice period.
- Where the employee works under a fixed-term contract, the date upon which that contract expires.

It should be noted for those employees dismissed and having just under 2 years' service that they are permitted in law to add to the end of the relevant termination date a period of one week. This represents the statutory minimum period of notice. If, in adding the 1 week, the employee then has 2 years' continuous service, they may claim their statutory redundancy payment.

6.4.2 THE REQUIREMENT OF DISMISSAL

The employee must have been dismissed. This may be deemed to have occurred in the following circumstances:

- The employer terminates the contract by issuing notice to the employee.
- The employer terminates the contract but does so summarily, without notice.
- The employee works under a fixed-term contract and that contract expires without being renewed.
- The employee terminates the contract with or without notice by reason of the employer's conduct. (Constructive dismissal situations).

There will be no dismissal and therefore no entitlement to statutory redundancy payment where:

- The employee's fixed-term contract is renewed.
- The employee is issued with a new contract of employment without there either being a break in service, or if there is a break, for a period of less than 4 weeks.
- The employee is offered a different job with the same or an associated employer and accepts the new position.
- The employee has resigned before notice of termination for redundancy has been issued to them by the employer.

With regard to the last point, it should be distinguished from the situation (as often happens) where the employer has issued notice of termination for redundancy and during that period of notice the employee leaves prematurely to take up alternative work. In these circumstances, the employee in question will normally remain entitled to statutory redundancy pay. However, if the employer objects to the employee's premature departure and serves on the employee a written request not to leave early, warning them that if they do so the employer will contest any liability to make a redundancy payment, they may lose their right to such payment. If the employer withholds the redundancy payment in these circumstances, the employee may apply to an employment tribunal. The tribunal will consider whether the employee's action in leaving prematurely was reasonable or unreasonable in the circumstances. An employee will not be entitled to any payment in lieu of notice for a period in which they were not ready, willing and able to work.

6.5 LAY-OFF AND SHORT-TIME WORKING

A redundancy situation in law can arise in cases of lay-off or short-time working imposed by the employer. The definitions of each are therefore important. An employee is deemed laid-off when the employer fails to provide work for the employee during a week under which a contract of employment is in existence. The employee must be available for work during such time. Short-time is where an employee receives less than half a week's work and pay during any week in which a contract of employment exists. Where these situations exist, subject to conditions, the employee may serve written notice on the employer for redundancy payment. The employee must have been:

- Laid-off or kept on short-time for 4 or more consecutive weeks; or
- Laid-off or kept on short-time for 6 weeks or more within a total of 13 weeks and not more than 3 of those 6 weeks were consecutive.

The employee must serve notice within 4 weeks of the last day of lay-off or short-time working to make their claim. If submitted by the employee, the employer may counter-claim where there is a reasonable expectation that within 4 weeks of the notice being served by the employee, full-time working will resume and continue for at least 13 weeks. The employer must serve this counter-notice in writing on the employee within 7 days of the employee's original notice.

If the employee disagrees with the reasonable expectation of work resuming made by the employer, they may have the situation determined by an employment tribunal and should not delay in processing their application in this regard. The employee must first terminate their contract of employment by giving contractual or statutory notice (1 week) to the employer – whichever is the greater.

No claim can be made for any week in which the lay-off or short-time working was as a result of employee's industrial action against the employer or due to the employer's imposed lock-out for similar reasons.

6.6 EXCLUDED EMPLOYEES

There are a number of circumstances in which an employee will be excluded from the basic right to a redundancy payment. These are listed as follows.

- Employees who have reached, or are over, the normal age of retirement for their employers. Or, where there is no express or implied normal retirement age, they have exceeded the age of 65. (This applies to both men and women).
- Share fishermen.
- Civil servants and other public employees.
- Employees who have accepted an offer from the employer of a suitable alternative job to that which was made redundant.
- Employees who have unreasonably refused to accept an offer, by their employer, of a suitable alternative job.
- Employees who initially accept alternative work as suitable, commence such work under a statutory trial period and unreasonably resign their position during that trial period.
- Employees who, during the period of notice of termination for redundancy, are dismissed for misconduct (given the short periods of notice that typically apply, most of these situations in practice involve the employee having committed an act of gross misconduct).

- Employees who, working under a fixed-term contract of employment, have agreed in writing with the employer, prior to commencement of work of two years or more under that contract, to exclude their right to claim a statutory payment in the event of a redundancy situation.
- Certain groups of employees affected by the operation of an exemption order as imposed by the government. This order may be made in respect of an employer and excludes them from liability for making statutory redundancy payments, where contractual terms are more advantageous to their employees.

6.7 TIME LIMIT FOR MAKING A CLAIM

If the employee believes that they are redundant and has made a claim to that effect in writing to their employer, but the employer refuses or fails to make due payment, the employee may apply to an employment tribunal for determination of the matter and payment. The application to the tribunal must be made within 6 months from the original claim to the employer or from when the employer has clearly refused to comply with the request. Where the employee is dismissed without payment, the employee must bring their claim within 6 months from the date of termination.

6.8 THE PAYMENT

The amount the employee receives as their statutory redundancy entitlement is dependent upon their age, length of service and gross weekly wage. Figure 1 provides a ready reckoner to calculate the payment. The amount payable is based on the following method of calculation.

- 1½ weeks' pay for each complete year of employment during which the employee was aged 41 or over but was less than 65 years of age or under the employer's normal retirement age where less than 65.
- 1 weeks' pay for each complete year of employment during which the employee was aged 22-40 inclusive.
- ½ weeks' pay for each complete year of employment in which the employee was aged 18-21 inclusive.
- Service before the employee's 18th birthday will not count.

Calculation is made by working backwards from the effective date of termination to take into account, first, those years of service which provide the greater entitlement. The calculation of 'a weeks' wage' is described in section 3.7 the amount is subject to a statutory ceiling of £230 per week. The maximum period of service taken into account is 20 years. The maximum payment is therefore currently £6,900. The ceiling figure of £230 per week is subject to annual review.

In the case of an employee being made redundant in their 64th year of age, the amount payable will fall to be reduced by one-twelfth for every complete month by which their age exceeds 64 years. This

Service (years)

Age (years)	2	3	4	5	6	7	8	9	10	11	12	13	14	15	16	17	18	19	20
20	1	1	1	1	–														
21	1	1½	1½	1½	1½	–													
22	1	1½	2	2	2	2	–												
23	1½	2	2½	3	3	3	3	–											
24	2	2½	3	3½	4	4	4	4	–										
25	2	3	3½	4	4½	5	5	5	5	–									
26	2	3	4	4½	5	5½	6	6	6	6	–								
27	2	3	4	5	5½	6	6½	7	7	7	7	–							
28	2	3	4	5	6	6½	7	7½	8	8	8	8	–						
29	2	3	4	5	6	7	7½	8	8½	9	9	9	9	–					
30	2	3	4	5	6	7	8	8½	9	9½	10	10	10	10	–				
31	2	3	4	5	6	7	8	9	9½	10	10½	11	11	11	11	–			
32	2	3	4	5	6	7	8	9	10	10½	11	11½	12	12	12	12	–		
33	2	3	4	5	6	7	8	9	10	11	11½	12	12½	13	13	13	13	–	
34	2	3	4	5	6	7	8	9	10	11	12	12½	13	13½	14	14	14	14	–
35	2	3	4	5	6	7	8	9	10	11	12	13	13½	14	14½	15	15	15	15
36	2	3	4	5	6	7	8	9	10	11	12	13	14	14½	15	15½	16	16	16
37	2	3	4	5	6	7	8	9	10	11	12	13	14	15	15½	16	16½	17	17
38	2	3	4	5	6	7	8	9	10	11	12	13	14	15	16	16½	17	17½	18
39	2	3	4	5	6	7	8	9	10	11	12	13	14	15	16	17	17½	18	18½
40	2	3	4	5	6	7	8	9	10	11	12	13	14	15	16	17	18	18½	19
41	2	3	4	5	6	7	8	9	10	11	12	13	14	15	16	17	18	19	19½
42	2½	3½	4½	5½	6½	7½	8½	9½	10½	11½	12½	13½	14½	15½	16½	17½	18½	19½	20½
43	3	4	5	6	7	8	9	10	11	12	13	14	15	16	17	18	19	20	21
44	3	4½	5½	6½	7½	8½	9½	10½	11½	12½	13½	14½	15½	16½	17½	18½	19½	20½	21½
45	3	4½	6	7	8	9	10	11	12	13	14	15	16	17	18	19	20	21	22
46	3	4½	6	7½	8½	9½	10½	11½	12½	13½	14½	15½	16½	17½	18½	19½	20½	21½	22½
47	3	4½	6	7½	9	10	11	12	13	14	15	16	17	18	19	20	21	22	23
48	3	4½	6	7½	9	10½	11½	12½	13½	14½	15½	16½	17½	18½	19½	20½	21½	22½	23½
49	3	4½	6	7½	9	10½	12	13	14	15	16	17	18	19	20	21	22	23	24
50	3	4½	6	7½	9	10½	12	13½	14½	15½	16½	17½	18½	19½	20½	21½	22½	23½	24½
51	3	4½	6	7½	9	10½	12	13½	15	16	17	18	19	20	21	22	23	24	25
52	3	4½	6	7½	9	10½	12	13½	15	16½	17½	18½	19½	20½	21½	22½	23½	24½	25½
53	3	4½	6	7½	9	10½	12	13½	15	16½	18	19	20	21	22	23	24	25	26
54	3	4½	6	7½	9	10½	12	13½	15	16½	18	19½	20½	21½	22½	23½	24½	25½	26½
55	3	4½	6	7½	9	10½	12	13½	15	16½	18	19½	21	22	23	24	25	26	27
56	3	4½	6	7½	9	10½	12	13½	15	16½	18	19½	21	22½	23½	24½	25½	26½	27½
57	3	4½	6	7½	9	10½	12	13½	15	16½	18	19½	21	22½	24	25	26	27	28
58	3	4½	6	7½	9	10½	12	13½	15	16½	18	19½	21	22½	24	25½	26½	27½	28½
59	3	4½	6	7½	9	10½	12	13½	15	16½	18	19½	21	22½	24	25½	27	28	29
60	3	4½	6	7½	9	10½	12	13½	15	16½	18	19½	21	22½	24	25½	27	28½	29½
61	3	4½	6	7½	9	10½	12	13½	15	16½	18	19½	21	22½	24	25½	27	28½	30
62	3	4½	6	7½	9	10½	12	13½	15	16½	18	19½	21	22½	24	25½	27	28½	30
63	3	4½	6	7½	9	10½	12	13½	15	16½	18	19½	21	22½	24	25½	27	28½	30
64	3	4½	6	7½	9	10½	12	13½	15	16½	18	19½	21	22½	24	25½	27	28½	30

Figure 1. Calculator for Statutory Redundancy Entitlement. (The figures represent the number of weeks pay to which the employee is entitled).

incremental reduction does not apply where the employer's normal retirement age is less than 65 years. Where an amount of statutory redundancy pay is payable it is not subject to tax or National Insurance deductions.

6.9 WRITTEN STATEMENT

The employee is entitled to receive from the employer a written statement as to how the redundancy payment has been calculated. There are two penalties for the employer's failure depending on the circumstances:

1. Where the employer fails to supply the statement they may be fined up to £200.
2. Where the employee has in writing requested a statement and the employer has failed to comply, they are liable to be fined up to £1,000.

These awards may be made by an employment tribunal upon application by the employee.

6.10 SUITABLE ALTERNATIVE EMPLOYMENT

The employer may be in a position to offer the redundant employee an alternative job within their business. If the alternative offered is 'suitable' it can entitle the employer to avoid liability for redundancy payments. Where it is suitable it may not be unreasonably refused by the employee. Two problem areas emerge.

1. When is an alternative job offer *suitable*?
2. What will be considered an *unreasonable* refusal?

When presenting the alternative position to the employee, the employer is under an obligation to clearly identify the new position and to set out the differences between it and the original job which is redundant. Only when this has been done will the employee be in a position to make a reasoned decision. The offer of the new role must be made before the existing contract of employment comes to an end and must take effect within 4 weeks of the expiry of the original contract. The employee is entitled to turn down the new job and state the reasons why they believe the position is unsuitable. There may be many reasons for unsuitability such as it:

*   Involves an inconvenient geographical relocation.
*   Involves greater travelling time to and from work.
*   Terms and conditions interfere with unavoidable or important family commitments.
*   Requires the employee to accept terms and conditions (e.g. hours, pay, holiday entitlement) which are less advantageous than the redundant position.

- Does not carry the level of status and responsibility which the employee enjoyed in their previous position.
- Requires considerable re-training.

(This list is not intended to be exhaustive).

Where reasons for unsuitability are put forward by the employee and they appear reasonable in the circumstances, a tribunal will be reluctant to force the employee to accept the alternative job offer. However, merely stating the offer is unsuitable without further supporting reasons, is unlikely to be acceptable. It follows that sound reasons for declining the job offered will allow the employee to be viewed as reasonably refusing the position. Although often borne out of the same facts, the issues of suitability and the reasonableness of refusal are looked at separately by the tribunal should the matter be put before them.

6.10.1 TRIAL PERIOD

Where an employer offers an alternative position and the new role involves a change to the existing terms and conditions of employment or is work of a different nature, the employee is entitled to request a 4 week trial period. The 4 weeks is a statutory period and may be extended by the parties with agreement. Whether 4 weeks or more the agreement must:

- Be in writing.
- Be made before the commencement of the trial period.
- Specify the date upon which the trial period is to end.
- State clearly the terms and conditions of employment which will apply at the end of the trial period.

The trial period can lead to three distinct situations.

1. If the employee is satisfied with the new role and continues after the expiry of the period they will have accepted the new position. There will be no dismissal in law, no entitlement to redundancy pay or notice and continuity of employment will be preserved.
2. At the end of the trial period the employee or employer may decide the role is unsuitable. Reasons for unsuitability must then be put forward. If the employer terminates the contract, the fairness of the dismissal will be assessed at the end of the trial period and not at the end of the original contract.
3. The employee may leave before the expiry of the trial period. In this situation the employee will be treated as having been dismissed on the date upon which their original contract came to an end.

The employee must be able to provide reasons for unsuitability, since failure to do so may be regarded as an unreasonable refusal of alternative work and disentitle them to a redundancy payment. The reason for termination will be regarded as the same reason for which the original contract was terminated; usually redundancy.

6.11 CHANGE OF EMPLOYER
Should the employer change further to the transfer of the business, this will not entitle any transferred employee to a statutory redundancy payment. This is because a transfer preserves continuity of employment and there will be no dismissal in law. Should the employee be made redundant shortly after transfer of the business by the new employer, they will be liable to pay the redundancy entitlement for the whole of the period of employment with both (or more) employers.

6.12 REDUNDANCY AND UNFAIR DISMISSAL
An employee may claim unfair dismissal by reason of redundancy before an employment tribunal provided they have 1 years' continuous service. Current legislation imposes on an employer a number of obligations when considering dismissal by reason of redundancy. Employees, therefore, have the right to be consulted prior to the decision to dismiss and not to be unfairly selected for redundancy. This section deals with those two issues in turn.

6.12.1 CONSULTATION – UNION AND/OR ELECTED EMPLOYEE REPRESENTATIVES
Not all employers recognise a trade union for the purposes of collective bargaining and they are under no general legal obligation to do so, unless the employees show their support by a majority joining a union or voting in favour of recognition in a specially organised ballot. Where they do, the employer is under a statutory duty to consult with that union where it is proposed to dismiss 20 or more employees, amongst the category of workers whom they represent, at one establishment within a period of 90 days or less. If an employer does not recognise a trade union, it must consult with the 'appropriate representatives' of the employees whom the employer is proposing to dismiss. The "appropriate representatives" may be either:

- Employee representatives already elected by the employees (provided that they are deemed to have the authority of the affected employees, bearing in mind the purpose for and method by which they were appointed or elected); or
- Employee representatives specifically elected for the purpose of collective redundancies.

The law sets out a number of criteria that must be satisfied in relation to an election of employee representatives. These include ensuring that all affected employees are entitled to vote and that none of the affected employees are unreasonably excluded from standing for election. The employees may vote for as many candidates as there are representatives to be elected to represent them. The voting process should be secret. The employer can determine the number of representatives to be elected (subject to ensuring that there are sufficient representatives to represent the interests of the affected employees) and their term of office (subject to enabling the consultation process to be properly completed). The employer can also decide whether the employees should be represented by a representative for a particular class of employees, or by representatives for the entire group.

Employees who participate in an election of employee representatives are entitled not to be dismissed, or subjected to a detriment, on that ground. In addition, employee representatives and trade union officials are entitled to time off during working hours for training to perform their functions in relation to consultation.

Where 'union consultation' is referred to in the rest of this section this should be read as including consultation with employee representative where appropriate. The employer must commence its consultation with the union as soon as redundancies are forecast. Consultation must in any event begin:

- Where 100 or more redundancies are proposed at one establishment within a 90 day period, at least 90 days before the first of the dismissals takes effect.
- Where 20 or more redundancies are proposed at least 30 days before the first dismissal takes effect.

Furthermore the employer must disclose in writing to the union representatives the following information:

- The reasons for the proposals.
- The number and descriptions of employees whom it is proposed to make redundant.
- The total number of employees of any such description employed by the employer at the establishment.
- The proposed method of selection.
- The proposed method of carrying out the dismissals with due regard to any agreed procedure.
- The proposed method of calculating the amount of any non-statutory redundancy payments.

The consultation must include exploration of ways to avoid the dismissals, reducing the number of employees to be dismissed and mitigating the consequences of the dismissals. Such consultation undertaken by the employer must be done so with a view to reaching agreement with the trade union representatives. The employer must consider and reply to any representations made by trade union representatives, giving reasons for any representations rejected. Should the union feel the employer has failed to meet these requirements it is entitled to make a complaint on behalf of its members to an employment tribunal. The tribunal is empowered to make a 'protective award' in favour of all employees within the relevant group. The amount of the award is one weeks' pay for each week of the 'protected period'. The length of the protected period is itself dependent upon how many employees it is proposed to make redundant at any one place of work. If the proposal is to dismiss:

- 100 or more employees = 90 days
- 20 or more employees = 30 days

The maximum protective award for failure to comply with the consultation obligations on collective redundancies is 90 days' pay for each employee. Finally, where collective redundancies are proposed, an employer must also send written notification in a prescribed form to the Department of Trade and Industry.

6.12.2 CONSULTATION – INDIVIDUAL EMPLOYEES

Regardless of whether they are a union member or one of many redundancies, each employee is entitled to be consulted individually prior to the decision to dismiss being made by the employer. The consultation must be meaningful with a view to fully exploring the possibility of avoiding the dismissal by some other agreed action between the parties. The consultation should discuss and explain to the employee the following key issues:

- The economic or business need for the proposed redundancy.
- The selection criteria used.
- The reasons why that individual has been provisionally selected for redundancy.
- Suitable alternative employment – if available.

Employees should be advised that the proposals are not finalised and invited to consider them and make any suggestions or comments they feel appropriate. It follows that such consultation will take time, at least several days and probably a week or more. Consultation does not mean the employer informing the employee that they are redundant and then asking for a response. The consultation must take place prior to the decision to implement dismissal by reason of redundancy. Failure to consult properly, or at all, will allow the employee to claim unfair dismissal before an employment tribunal.

6.12.3 SELECTION

Unfair selection for redundancy can lead to an unfair dismissal. The tribunal will not hesitate to scrutinize a selection decision where it appears to contravene the custom and practice of the business or contractual procedures and where there was no special reason for justifying a departure from such arrangements. Selection for redundancy should be in accordance with agreed procedures where they exist. Where they do not, custom and practice should be followed which invariably is, 'last in, first out,'(LIFO). The order of priority is therefore:

- Agreed contractual procedure – written or oral.
- Custom and practice.

Once the correct procedure is identified it should be applied in conjunction with the necessary consultation process. Where LIFO is the criterion for selection, care should be taken in assessing the length of service. The employee is entitled to count the length of continuous employment only, rather than cumulative periods of service with breaks between each. Also, a series of fixed-term contracts renewed without due formality could constitute a single unbroken period of employment for the purposes of LIFO.

The application of an agreed procedure does not have to be implemented 'across the board' by the employer. It may be restricted to that area(s) of the business where manning cuts are necessary. The employer must not only consider the job descriptions of the employees concerned but also what functions those employees perform in practice. The employer may wish to deviate from an agreed or customary procedure. To do this they will require special reasons. Cases on 'special reasons' indicate that the following factors may be acceptable:

- Skills.
- Experience.
- Qualifications.

The employer may consider the above both in contemplating what they require at the time of the decision to dismiss for redundancy and what they reasonably believe will be their requirements in the future. Any criteria used must be objective and verifiable by reference to data such as attendance records, length of service, measurable efficiency and skills audits.

Finally, employees should be aware that any attempt to select them for redundancy based on vague subjective criteria such as quality of work, inter-personal skills or attitude are, on their own, very likely to be regarded as unfair. An employer cannot use redundancy as a 'convenient' method of dismissal and remove an individual from their employment for this reason when they are otherwise disenchanted with their performance. Performance problems must be dealt with by using a disciplinary procedure. Redundancy will stand or fall on its own economic facts and circumstances. The conduct of the employee, past and present, should never be used as a single criterion for selection by the employer. Where an employee feels that this is occurring they should not hesitate to issue proceedings before an employment tribunal for unfair dismissal, having first exhausted all internal avenues of grievance.

6.13 CASE STUDY

John owns an ornamental plant centre and is experiencing trading difficulties. He specialises in palm trees and it has been a particularly wet summer. The public, seemingly, do not want to buy his stock of exotic trees. Claire is 26 years old, earns £240.00 a week and has been working for John for 6 years. She is one of only three staff at the centre who all do similar work and have similar skills, qualifications and experience. Out of the 3 staff, Claire has the shortest service.

John is aware that if business does not get better soon he will have to make one of his staff redundant. He is aware of the requirement for consultation and at a meeting with all his staff informs them that a redundancy in the future may be a possibility.

Claire is alarmed at this news. She panics, looks for another job the next day and accepts an offer of employment with a local florist on lower pay. She tenders her resignation to John in writing stating she is willing to work 1 weeks' notice and that she looks forward to receiving her statutory redundancy pay. John seeks legal advice.

Claire is not entitled to statutory redundancy pay. The reason being she was not dismissed for redundancy and resigned before John issued formal notice of redundancy. John had only just begun the consultation process. If Claire had secured alternative employment after formal notice of redundancy had been issued, she would have been entitled to resign within the notice period and statutory redundancy pay would have been payable had John not objected to her premature departure. Given her age, gross weekly wage and length of service her redundancy entitlement would have been as follows.

5 x £230 (maximum weekly wage)
£1,150 — tax free.

Claire's impatience cost her dearly.

DISCIPLINARY PRACTICE AND PROCEDURE

7.1 THE REQUIREMENT

It is a common theme running through UK law that nobody should be punished unjustly for an act or omission that was not their responsibility. Employment law is no exception. To be disciplined for an act of misconduct can have a grave effect on the employee concerned. At best, it acts as a 'blot on the copy-book' and at worst it could lead to dismissal. It follows that the law requires certain procedures to be closely followed by employers before any disciplinary sanction may reasonably be imposed on the employee concerned. Failure on the part of the employer will allow the employee to claim unfair dismissal before an employment tribunal where they have more than 1 years' continuous service.

According to ACAS, disciplinary rules and procedures are necessary for promoting fairness and order in the treatment of individuals and in the conduct of industrial relations. They also assist an organisation to operate effectively. Rules set standards of conduct at work; procedures help to ensure that the standards are adhered to and also provide a fair method of dealing with alleged failures to observe them. It is therefore vital that employees know what standards of conduct are expected of them. The law requires employers, in the written particulars of employment, to provide information about certain aspects of their disciplinary rules and procedures.

The importance of disciplinary rules and procedures has also been recognised in law in respect of dismissals, since the grounds for dismissal and the way in which the dismissal has been handled can be challenged before an employment tribunal. Where either of these is found by a tribunal to be unfair the employer may be guilty of unfair dismissal and ordered to reinstate or re-engage the employee concerned and may be liable to pay compensation to them.

ACAS have produced two publications, the 1997 Code of Practice on Disciplinary Practice and Procedures in Employment and the advisory handbook, 'Discipline at Work'. Both publications provide detailed practical advice on the formulation and operation of disciplinary procedures (for the offices of ACAS – see Useful Addressees). The aim of the ACAS documents is to help employers, trade unions and individual employees wherever they are employed, and regardless of the size of the organisation in which they work. In smaller establishments it may not be practicable to adopt all the detailed provisions, but most of the features listed later in this chapter could and should be adopted by employers and incorporated into a simple procedure.

7.2 FORMULATING POLICY

The ACAS Code of Practice clearly states that it is management who are responsible for maintaining discipline within an organisation and for ensuring that there are adequate disciplinary rules and procedures. The initiative for establishing these will normally lie with the management. However, if they are to be fully effective, the rules and procedures used need to be accepted as reasonable by those employees who are to be covered by them and those who operate them. Management should therefore aim to secure the involvement of employees and all levels of management when formulating new or revising existing rules and procedures.

7.2.1 RULES

It is unlikely that any set of disciplinary rules can cover all circumstances that arise. The rules required will necessarily vary according to particular circumstances such as:

* Type of work.
* Working conditions.
* The size of the employer.

When the employer draws up the rules they must have a mind to specifying clearly and concisely those necessary for the efficient and safe performance of work and for the maintenance of satisfactory relations within the workforce and between the employees and management. Rules should not be so general as to be meaningless.

Rules should be readily available and the employer should make every effort to ensure that employees know and understand them. ACAS suggest that this may be achieved by giving every employee a copy of the rules and by explaining them orally. In the case of new employees this should form part of an induction programme. Finally, employees should be made aware of the likely consequences of breaking rules and in particular they should be given a clear indication of the type of conduct that may warrant summary dismissal.

7.3 ESSENTIAL FEATURES OF DISCIPLINARY PROCEDURES

In their code of practice, ACAS indicate what should comprise a good and effective disciplinary procedure. They also state that procedures should not be viewed primarily as a means of imposing sanctions against an employee. They should also be designed to emphasise and encourage improvement in individual conduct. The disciplinary procedures should:

* Be in writing.
* Specify to whom they apply.
* Provide for matters to be dealt with quickly.
* Indicate the disciplinary actions that may be taken.
* Specify the levels of management that may have the authority to take the various forms of disciplinary action, ensuring that

immediate superiors do not normally have the power to dismiss without reference to senior management.

- Provide for individuals to be informed of the complaints against them and to be given the opportunity to state their case before decisions are reached.
- Give individuals the right to be accompanied by a trade union representative or a fellow employee of their choice. (This is now a statutory right).
- Ensure that no employees are dismissed for a first breach of discipline, except for gross misconduct.
- Ensure that disciplinary action is not taken until the case has been carefully investigated.
- Ensure that individuals are given an explanation for any penalty imposed.
- Provide a right of appeal and specify the procedure to be followed.

Employees must be aware that, generally, the Code of Practice is not law. Its importance lies in it being admissible as evidence before an employment tribunal and that in practice tribunals would like its provisions to be closely followed by employers. Where they are not followed and there is no good reason, a finding of unfair dismissal is likely. That is to say, a failure to follow a procedure prescribed in the Code can make an otherwise fair dismissal, unfair.

7.4 THE PROCEDURE IN OPERATION

According to ACAS the employee should expect the implementation of the following procedure:

> *When a disciplinary matter arises, the supervisor or manager should first establish the facts promptly, before recollections fade, taking into account the statements of any available witnesses. In a serious case, such as where there is a reasonable belief that an act of gross misconduct has taken place, it may be necessary for the employer to suspend the employee while the case is investigated. Unless there is a provision in the contract of employment to the contrary, this period of suspension should be on full pay. The period of suspension should be for no longer than is reasonably necessary in the circumstances. It cannot be used by the employer as an excuse to do nothing more. That would be unfair on the employee who in all probability will be keen for an outcome, good or bad.*

Before any decision is made by the employer or any penalty imposed against the employee, the individual should be interviewed and given the opportunity to state their case. The employee should   be advised of their statutory right to have a trade union representative or colleague from the workplace present at the hearing. Where the facts of the case appear to call for disciplinary action, other than summary dismissal, the following procedure should normally be observed:

1. In the case of minor offences the individual should be given a formal oral warning. It is recommended that the warning be confirmed in writing.
2. If the misconduct continues or the first offence is more serious, the employee should receive a first written warning. This warning should set out the nature of the offence and the likely consequences of further offences. In either case, the individual should be advised that the warning constitutes a formal stage of the disciplinary procedure.
3. Should further similar misconduct occur, the employer may issue a final written warning. This should contain a statement that any recurrence will lead to either dismissal or some other penalty.
4. Should similar misconduct continue, the final stage of the procedure is the implementation of dismissal, disciplinary transfer or disciplinary suspension according to the nature of the misconduct (but in the case of the latter two, only if these are allowed for by an express term of the employment contract). Periods of disciplinary suspension without pay should not normally be for prolonged periods of time.

In summary, the procedure which an employee guilty of misconduct other than gross misconduct can expect is one of four stages:

1. Oral warning.
2. First written warning.
3. Final written warning.
4. Dismissal.

At each stage the employee should be told of any right of appeal, how to make it and to whom.

There must be a fair hearing prior to the implementation of each stage. The employer must not prejudge the situation. Classic examples of prejudgment which may render the warning invalid are where the employer:

1. Without consultation sends the warning by post to the employee.
2. Holds a disciplinary hearing only to hand a pre-written warning to the employee at the end of the meeting.

A reasonable period of time should elapse between each warning to allow the employee an opportunity to improve and for the employer to properly monitor the employee's performance. What is a reasonable lapse of time is not defined in law but will depend on the facts of the case and the type of misconduct or poor performance. For example, instances of insubordination may be met with a different stage of the disciplinary procedure on each occasion. A general complaint of poor performance would have to be monitored over a period of time to allow any meaningful analysis of improvement or continued unsatisfactory work.

Employers are not generally entitled to progress on to the next stage of the procedure where a substantially different type of misconduct has occurred from the original warning. For example, it would be unfair for the employer to issue a final written warning for poor workmanship, if the employee is in receipt of a verbal warning and first written warning for poor time-keeping. The correct procedure would be to issue a verbal warning for the unsatisfactory level of performance. The employee in that example would then be on a first written warning for time-keeping and a verbal warning for performance. The law expects employers to recognise this differential.

7.5 EXCEPTIONAL CASES

There are certain situations where special consideration should be given to the way in which disciplinary procedures are to operate.

7.5.1 TRADE UNION OFFICIALS

Disciplinary action against a trade union official can lead to a serious dispute at the workplace if it is seen as an attack on the union's functions. Whilst not exempt from and clearly subject to normal disciplinary standards, no disciplinary action beyond an oral warning should be taken until the circumstances of the case have been discussed with a senior trade union representative or full-time official.

7.5.2 CRIMINAL OFFENCES OUTSIDE EMPLOYMENT

There may be occasions when an employee commits a criminal offence away from the work place out of work time. These should not be treated as automatic reasons for dismissal. The employer must have due regard to whether the offence has any relevance to the duties of the individual as an employee. The main considerations should be whether the offence is one that has undermined the relationship of trust and confidence between the parties or made the individual unsuitable for their type of work or unacceptable to other employees. Employees should not be dismissed solely because a charge against them is pending or because they are absent through having been remanded in custody.

7.5.3 EMPLOYEES IN PARTICULAR WORKING ENVIRONMENTS

Special provisions may have to be made for the handling of disciplinary matters among nightshift workers, or those in isolated locations or work sites, since there may be no one present with the necessary authority to take disciplinary action or no trade union representative available. Employees in these working environments are still entitled to be treated fairly and reasonably.

7.6 INVESTIGATION

Before an employer may reasonably make a decision as to whether or not an employee deserves to be disciplined, a full investigation of the facts is important. The employer cannot act against an employee on the basis of mere suspicion and should treat with great caution matters of hearsay. The employer must have an honest and genuine belief, based on some proof, after all reasonable investigation, that the employee is guilty of the alleged misconduct. Reasonable investigation is a necessary ingredient of any fair disciplinary process.

The employer is under a duty to gather together all available evidence. Possession of the facts should precede a reasonable decision as to what action (if any) is necessary. A good example of where an employer has failed to undertake proper investigation is when they present the employee with a general allegation of misconduct unsupported by references to incidents or events. When faced with a 'blanket' allegation, an employee is entitled to reply with a 'blanket' denial. This will not be held against them by a tribunal. The employer must, well in advance of any disciplinary hearing, provide the employee with specific details relating to the allegation, including the following information where reasonably practicable:

- Date.
- Time.
- Place.
- The people involved.
- The witnesses.
- All facts relevant to the act of misconduct.
- Why the incident is regarded as misconduct by the employer.
- If the employer regards the misconduct as potentially gross in nature, this must be made clear to the employee.

Ideally, this information should be given to the employee in writing, both to avoid doubt and for future reference.

The employer should not unnecessarily delay the disciplinary proceedings in undertaking investigation. There is a balance to be struck between having possession of most of the facts and acting promptly before recollections fade. Where the period of investigation is seen to be unnecessarily lengthy and the employee is subsequently dismissed, a claim of unfair dismissal may be possible. The employee must show that the employer's delay in implementing the disciplinary procedure was prejudicial, e.g. the evidence was stale, witnesses were not available or specific detail was insufficient.

The employer must undertake investigation at the earliest opportunity that will usually be as soon as they become aware of the facts. Failure to act promptly will allow the employee a claim for unfair dismissal, since to be aware of the conduct and to do nothing may be viewed as the employer's acceptance that such conduct is permitted in the employee's performance of their duties.

In conducting the investigation, witnesses should be interviewed and statements taken. The employer need not interview every available witness once the facts surrounding the misconduct have been clearly established. Should the employer overlook a key witness the investigation may be flawed. Where the evidence of a witness is used against an employee, as a general rule the employee is entitled to question the witness as part of the disciplinary process if they wish. The employee is allowed to do this in order to test the accuracy of the witness' account of events and to establish whether there exists any ulterior motive for the allegation. The problem is complicated where the witness or informant wishes to remain anonymous and the employee at the centre of the allegation is thereby potentially disadvantaged. In such situations the courts have provided the following guidelines to ensure a fair hearing whilst protecting the request for anonymity:

- The informant's statement should be reduced to writing in full.
- In taking this statement the employer must note the date, time and place of each observation or incident and the informant's opportunity to observe clearly and accurately.
- The employer should consider whether the informant had any reason to fabricate evidence.
- Having taken the statement, the employer should then undertake further investigation with a view to finding other independent supporting evidence.
- Enquiries should be made into the character and background of the informant.
- A decision must then be made as to whether to hold a disciplinary hearing.
- If possible, the informant should be personally interviewed by the employer with a view to deciding what weight should be given to their evidence.
- The informant's statement should be made available to the employee and their representative in advance of the disciplinary hearing.
- Should the employee or their representative have any reasonable questions to ask the informant, wherever practicable the employer should accommodate a request and refer back with answers.
- Careful notes should be taken at disciplinary hearing where informants are involved.

Employees faced with allegations based on the evidence of an informant have no legal right to demand to question them. However, an employee is entitled to request that the employer adheres to a procedure, as outlined above.

7.7 CRIMINAL PROCEEDINGS PENDING

Where it is alleged that the employee has committed a criminal act, inside or outside the workplace, and the police are proceeding with a prosecution, this can cause problems for the internal disciplinary hearing. In such circumstances, it is rarely acceptable for the employer to do nothing until the outcome of the criminal hearing. They should do their best to come to a decision as to the employee's guilt and whether, if at all, this affects the employment relationship. This requires a hearing to be held and a decision to be made. If the decision is to dismiss the employee and, this is implemented and then the employee is acquitted of the criminal charge, the dismissal will not necessarily be unfair. Fairness will depend on the procedure adopted and the facts available to the employer at the time of the decision.

7.8 STANDARD OF PROOF

Employees must be clear that the purpose of a fair disciplinary process is to ensure that the employer comes to a reasonable decision on the facts of the case. The employer is not required to prove the case against the employee beyond all reasonable doubt. That requirement is for the criminal courts and has no place in a civil employment environment. The employer is required to be satisfied on the 'balance of probabilities' that the employee acted as alleged. That is, on the evidence available, having investigated the facts and heard the employee's story, it was more probable than not that the employee committed the alleged misconduct. Provided the employer satisfies this standard of proof any subsequent dismissal will be potentially fair.

7.9 THE DISCIPLINARY HEARING

Having decided to proceed with a disciplinary hearing the employer must conduct such proceedings fairly in the interests of 'natural justice'. This is deemed necessary because a person's job is at stake. A serious breach of the rules of natural justice will make a dismissal unfair.

7.9.1 THE EMPLOYEE STATES THEIR CASE

The purpose of a hearing is twofold:

1. To investigate whether or not misconduct has been committed.
2. To allow the employee to put forward a reason or explanation for their conduct.

The employee must be given an opportunity to state their version of events and put forward any mitigating circumstances. What may seem obvious misconduct to the employer may have a perfectly innocent explanation. For example, in one well-known case, the employee was dismissed for allegedly being in a 'drunken state'. If the employers had allowed the employee an opportunity to explain, they would have discovered that his 'state' was due to medication for toothache. The dismissal was held unfair.

Only in extraordinary cases may an employer not hear the employee's side of events and the dismissal still be regarded as fair where the employee is not willing to attend the hearing. Furthermore, the employee should be given an opportunity to speak to the person who will actually make the disciplinary decision. The decision-maker should not hear of the case third-hand. Should the employee be given the opportunity to explain their conduct but fail to do so, a subsequent dismissal will be potentially fair.

7.9.2 DETAILS OF THE ALLEGATION

As stated earlier in section 7.6, the employee should know of the case against them well in advance of the hearing. This is to allow them to prepare and present a defence. The employer who 'springs' a disciplinary hearing on an employee may well invalidate the proceedings. Moreover, once the employee has been given details prior to a hearing, there should be no 'surprise' new allegations added at the hearing itself. If there are, the employee would be acting reasonably in declining to comment and requesting an adjournment of the hearing in order to prepare a proper defence. Any evidence upon which the employer is seeking to rely in making the allegations must be given in advance to the employee. The allegations and their specific facts will be the focus of the disciplinary hearing. Where witness evidence is being used, the witness must be made available for questioning at the hearing if the employee so requests. The hearing itself should not be over-formal. It is not a court of law but rather a forum for questioning by both employer and employee and for general investigation.

7.9.3 THE DECISION-MAKER

Where the resources of the business allow, the person investigating the misconduct on behalf of the employer should not be the decision-maker. The investigator should assemble evidence to be put before another person - the decision-maker. This is to avoid a formed opinion of the investigator from wrongly interfering with the objective assessment of the facts, which should be undertaken by the decision-maker in the interests of fair-play. In addition the decision-maker should not have a direct interest in the outcome of the disciplinary hearing. If they did, there would exist an unfair bias against the employee. The chances of bias should be minimised by the employer whenever reasonably practicable.

7.9.4 REPRESENTATION

The employer does not have to allow an employee to be legally represented. After all, this is an internal disciplinary hearing not a court of law. However, if the contract of employment states that the employee, "has the right to be represented" (or words to that effect) the employee may ask for their solicitor or other advocate to state their defence to the allegations. In any event, a worker attending a disciplinary or grievance hearing has a statutory right to be accompanied by a union representative or fellow employee of their choice. The individual must be:

- Selected by the employee.
- Permitted to address the hearing (but not to answer questions on the employee's behalf).
- Permitted to confer with the employee during the hearing.

Whilst the employer is free to select an initial date for the hearing, they are required to re-schedule a hearing where the employee's chosen companion is not available on the date proposed for the hearing by the employer. The employee must propose an alternative time which is reasonable and which falls within a period of five working days (excluding weekends and Bank Holidays), beginning with the first working days after the day proposed by the employer. The employee's companion must be given time off during working hours to accompany the employee for these purposes.

An employee may complain to an employment tribunal where an employer has not allowed a companion to attend a hearing or where the employer has failed to re-schedule a hearing. The tribunal can order an employer to pay compensation of up to a maximum of two weeks' pay to the employee.

7.9.5 THE DECISION

Only in very clear-cut cases should the employee expect a decision at the end of the hearing. Usually the decision will follow some time after the hearing has been concluded. The employer is under an obligation before making a decision to bear in mind all relevant factors. The ACAS Code of Practice states the relevant factors are:

- The employee's general record, age, position and length of service.
- Whether the disciplinary procedure indicates what the likely penalty will be as a result of the particular misconduct.
- The penalty imposed in similar cases in the past.
- Any special circumstances, e.g. provocation.
- Any mitigating factors, e.g. the employee's health or domestic situation.
- The gravity of the offence.
- The range of sanctions available within the disciplinary procedure.

7.10 APPEALS

Where the contract of employment provides for an appeal procedure it should be followed. Where there is no contractual appeal, failure to allow one may be grounds to claim unfair dismissal. An appeal procedure should clarify:

- The time period within which the appeal must be lodged.
- To whom the appeal should be made.
- Whether the appeal should be oral or submitted in writing only.
- Whose decision is final.
- How that decision will be communicated.
- The time period within which the decision will be made.

Once more, depending on the resources available to the employer, the appeal should be heard by someone other than the first decision-maker to allow an objective review of the facts and circumstances of the case.

The conduct of the appeal hearing and the composition of the appeal 'panel' is therefore important. Unless otherwise stated, the contract of employment will be effectively terminated at the point in time when the original decision to dismiss is communicated to the employee. The contract will not remain live until the outcome of the appeal. If the appeal is successful and overturns the decision to dismiss, then the employee will be treated as having been suspended pending the outcome of the appeal. Impliedly such suspension will be with pay unless there exists a contractual provision to the contrary.

Finally, it should be noted that where an employee has failed to make use of an available appeal procedure offered by the employer following dismissal, an employment tribunal has the power to reduce any unfair dismissal compensatory award by up to two weeks' pay. Similarly, if the employer denies access to an appeal, compensation may be increased by up to two weeks' pay.

7.11 THE IMPORTANCE OF LENGTH OF SERVICE

The ACAS Code of Practice on disciplinary procedures is not law. However it is well established that breach of the Code may well render a dismissal unfair. In Chapter 4 it is explained that in order to claim unfair dismissal before an employment tribunal the employee must have one years' continuous service. Without that length of service, no matter how blatant the breach of the Code or how unfair the dismissal, the employee cannot challenge the decision on its merits. The employee will only be able to claim for money owed under the contract of employment in a wrongful dismissal claim.

If, however, the contract of employment is so worded that the disciplinary procedure (if any) outlined within it is contractually binding from day one of the commencement of employment, it follows that an employer's subsequent failure to follow the procedure will be a breach of contract. Where the employer is in breach of contract the employee is entitled to claim damages before an employment tribunal or county court. Damages should be assessed on the basis of the amount of wages or salary that would have been earned by the employee had the employer gone through the disciplinary procedure in the contract, subject to the employee's duty to mitigate their loss and actively seek employment elsewhere. To date, claims such as these are few in practice. But there is nothing, in theory, to prevent such a claim. It may be worth a try, particularly before an employment tribunal where the procedure for application is simple and there is so little to lose.

7.12 RECORDS AND DATA PROTECTION

The employer is obliged to keep records detailing the nature of any breach of disciplinary rules, the action taken and the reasons for it. Details of appeals, where lodged by the employee, should also be kept. The employer should keep these records safely and confidentially.

After a period of time, a warning will become lapsed and may be disregarded. Where the contract of employment says nothing about the duration of warning, the normal common law rule is that it will lapse after a period of 1 year. The contract or the warning itself may state a shorter period of time. If longer than one year the contract term may be challenged as unreasonable and if an employee is dismissed as a result of its application, it may be claimed to be unfair before an employment tribunal. The importance of a warning having lapsed is that in the event of further similar misconduct by the employee, the employer will have to 'go back' to the preceding live warning, if any.

Under the Data Protection Act 1998, which came into force in March 2000, employees have the right to receive a copy of their personnel files on request and to demand that any inaccuracies be corrected or removed. They also have the right to be told whether and for what purposes personal information relating to them is being processed, the nature of the data and the people to whom the information may be disclosed.

It is important to note at the outset that transitional provisions set out in the Act give employers a period of several years to comply with the new provisions in relation to existing paper-based records. However, most employers will want to start reviewing their existing arrangements as soon as possible.

The extension of the data protection provisions to cover paper-based records is likely to have significant implications for many employers. In many cases, the first step is to carry out an audit of what paper information is held, where it is located and the purposes for which it is used.

7.12.1 THE PRINCIPLES

The Act contains eight basic principles:

1. Personal data shall be processed fairly and lawfully and shall not be processed unless certain conditions are met in relation to personal data and additional conditions in relation to sensitive personal data. The conditions are:

    *   The data subject has given his consent to the processing, or
    *   The processing is necessary for the various purposes set out in the Act.

2. Personal data shall be obtained only for one or more specified and lawful purposes. Personal data shall not be processed in any manner incompatible with that purpose or those purposes.

3. Personal data shall be adequate, relevant and not excessive in relation to the purpose or purposes for which they are processed. The personnel files of long-serving employees may contain a backlog of out-of-date or irrelevant information. Employers would therefore be well advised to review their personnel files periodically to ensure that there is a sound business reason requiring the information to be held.

4. Personal data shall be accurate and, where necessary, kept up to date. One way of ensuring compliance with the fourth principle is for employers to provide employees with a copy of their personnel files at regular intervals, and to set up a mechanism whereby employees can raise queries and notify any changes to the information stored.

5. Personal data processed for any purpose or purposes shall not be kept for longer than is necessary for that purpose or those purposes. One of the key issues in relation to employment is the length of time for which personnel records should be retained after the employee has left their employment. The minimum period of time for which an employer will want to preserve a personnel record is until any potential legal action by the ex-employee would be time-barred. In the case of an unfair dismissal claim the period is three months, but in the case of action for injury sustained at work the period is three years – or longer still if the injury is not apparent when the employee leaves. In respect of breach of contract claims, they are actionable within six years.

6. Personal data shall be processed in accordance with the rights of data subjects under the Act.

7. Appropriate technical and organisational measures shall be taken against unauthorised or unlawful processing of personal data and against accidental loss or destruction of, or damage to, data. Employers may be expected to adopt computerised back-up procedures, and to ensure that only authorised persons within the organisation have access to employee data. Data should not be removed from its normal place of storage without good reason.

8. Personal data shall not be transferred to a country or territory outside the European Economic Area unless that country or territory ensures an adequate level of protection for the rights and freedoms of data subjects in relation to the processing of personal data.

7.12.2 DEFINITIONS

Relevant Filing System. A 'relevant filing system' is defined as a set of non-automated information relating to individuals which is 'structured, either by reference to individuals or by reference to criteria relating to individuals, in such a way that specific information relating to a particular individual is readily accessible'.

The Government has suggested that a 'relevant filing system' would include 'files about named individuals in which each item has an internal structure conforming to some common system'. For example, files with the subject's name or another unique personal identifier on the cover, and containing one or more pro forma documents. It is likely, therefore, that paper-based personnel records that form part of an organised filing system will come within the scope of the new data protection provisions.

Personal Data. This is defined as data relating to a living individual and includes within the definition 'any expression of opinion about the individual'.

Processing. Principle 1 regards the 'processing' of personal data. The term 'processing' includes:

- Organising, adapting or altering data.
- Retrieving, consulting or use of the data.
- Disclosure of the data by any means.
- Erasing or destroying the data.

Sensitive Personal Data. In addition, 'sensitive personal data' may only be processed with the 'explicit consent' of the data subject and consists of information relating to:

- Race or ethnic origin.
- Political opinions, trade union membership.
- Religious or other beliefs.
- Physical or mental health or condition.
- Sexual life.
- Criminal offences, both committed and alleged.

Data Controller. The 'data controller' is a person who determines the purpose for which and the manner in which any personal data are processed. There may be several 'data controllers'. An employer is a 'data controller' for the purpose of the Act.

Data Subject. In the context of employment this will include any employee.

Exemptions. There are a number of exemptions from the data protection regime set out in the Act, e.g.:

- Confidential references (including those given by and to employers).
- Management forecasts (probably including documents setting out management plans for an employee's future development and progress).
- Documents subject to legal professional privilege.

7.12.3 ACCESS AND INFORMATION

Under the Act, employees have the right, on request:

- To be told by the employer whether personal data about them is being processed.

- To be given a description of the data concerned, the purposes for which it is being processed, and the recipients or classes of recipients to whom it is or may be disclosed.
- To have communicated 'in an intelligible form' the personal data concerned, and any information available to the employer as to the source of the data.
- To be informed in certain circumstances of the logic involved in computerised decision-making.

The employer is not obliged to supply the information mentioned above unless the employee has made a written request and has paid a fee, currently £10. The employer must comply with the request within 40 days.

7.12.4 CORRECTION OF INACCURATE DATA

An employee has the right under the Act to apply to the High Court or to a county court on the grounds that the personal data relating to them is inaccurate. If the complaint is upheld, the court may order the employer to rectify, block, erase or destroy that data and any other personal data that contains an expression of opinion based on the inaccurate information. If the inaccurate data has been disclosed to third parties, the court may also order the employer to notify those third parties that the inaccurate information has been corrected.

7.12.5 NOTIFICATION

The Act introduces a simplified system of 'notification' of information in place of the registration scheme that existed under the earlier legislation. The details that an employer will be obliged to notify under the Act include; a description of the personal data being processed and of the category or categories of data subject to which it relates, the purposes for which the data is being processed, and any person to whom the employer intends to disclose the data.

7.12.6 ENFORCEMENT

The Act confers extensive powers of enforcement, including powers of entry and inspection, on the Data Protection Commissioner. If a data controller has contravened the data protection principles, the Commissioner may issue an enforcement notice. The Commissioner may also issue a notice requiring the data controller to provide information for the purpose of determining whether a data protection principle has been breached. Failure to comply with a notice amounts to a criminal offence. Individuals may also apply to the Commissioner in certain circumstances for an assessment as to whether the provisions of the Act have been complied with, and in many instances they will be able to recover compensation from the data controller if a breach has taken place.

7.12.7 IMPLEMENTATION

For paper-based personnel files the following will apply:

- 'New' processing i.e. Processing commencing on or after 24 October 1998, is subject to all relevant provisions and to each of the 8 principles.
- 'Old' processing i.e. Processing already underway immediately before 24 October 1998, is exempt until 23 October 2001 from each of the 8 principles and from the provisions governing employees' rights of access and right to correct inaccurate data and exempt from principles 1-5 (only) until 23 October 2007.

7.13 CASE STUDY

Phillipa is a sales representative for Nisrine Cosmetics Limited. She has four years service and spends much of her time on the road in her own car visiting existing and potential clients. Under her contract of employment, she is entitled to claim a mileage allowance of 31 pence per mile.

A fellow employee of Phillipa's informs Matthew, the Sales and Marketing Manager, that he believes Phillipa is 'fiddling' her mileage expenses. The informant wishes to remain anonymous. Matthew is incensed by the hearsay and calls Phillipa into his office. When Phillipa arrives, he tells her the meeting constitutes a disciplinary hearing and puts the allegations of 'expense fiddling' to her. Phillipa is shocked and denies the allegation. Matthew provides expense claim forms that he believes support the allegation against her. Phillipa continues to deny the alleged misconduct. Matthew terminates the 'hearing' by handing Phillipa a letter confirming her dismissal for gross misconduct. The letter was written prior to the 'hearing'. Phillipa is distraught and seeks legal advice.

Phillipa is advised to claim unfair dismissal before an employment tribunal on the basis that the procedure prior to implementing the dismissal is seriously flawed in law. The main faults are as follows:

- Phillipa should have been consulted and suspended on full pay (as a neutral act) pending further investigation by Matthew.

- The allegations of the informant should have been detailed in writing and presented to Phillipa in advance of any hearing along with the supporting evidence of the expense claims forms. This would have allowed Phillipa a proper opportunity to prepare a defence.
- The blanket allegation put to Phillipa by Matthew was justly met with a blanket denial. The disciplinary hearing should have been properly convened with Phillipa being given advance written notice of the allegations and evidence against her.
- Either Phillipa should have been given the opportunity to personally cross-examine the informant or less weight and credibility should have been attached to his evidence by Matthew if the informant would not agree to this.
- Phillipa should have been given the opportunity of being accompanied at the hearing by a trade union representative or a colleague of her choice.
- If at all practicable given the resources of the employer, Matthew should not have acted as investigator and decision-maker.
- Handing Phillipa a letter at the end of the 'hearing' confirming her dismissal was an act of pre-judgment.
- Phillipa's claim is successful and the tribunal awarded her £7,000 compensation for unfair dismissal.

CHAPTER EIGHT
DISCRIMINATION

8.1 RECOGNISED DISCRIMINATION
Presently UK employment law recognises the following types of discrimination: sex, part-time, race and disability. This chapter will deal with each type in turn.

8.2 SEX DISCRIMINATION
The Sex Discrimination Act 1975 provides that women and men may bring claims of discrimination on the grounds of their sex or marital status or if victimised on those same grounds. It follows that a person may be discriminated against in one of three ways:

1. Directly.
2. Indirectly.
3. Via victimisation.

Indeed, most sex discrimination claims of whatever type are brought by women. For that reason, this section will concentrate on the unlawful discrimination against women, although men may apply if similar discrimination is evident.

8.2.1 DIRECT DISCRIMINATION
This occurs where a woman, on the grounds of her sex, is treated less favourably than a man or if married is treated less favourably than a single person. Any woman making such a claim must be able to show that not only is her treatment different but that it is also unfavourable. The latter is a key ingredient. A typical example of direct discrimination is where a female employee is told by her employer that she would have been promoted but for her being a woman. The test applied by the courts is, therefore, would the employee have been treated more favourably 'but for' her sex. The main examples of direct discrimination are as follows:

- A female employee who applies for a job is not offered the position because the employer's conclusion is that they would have offered them the position but for their sex.
- A female employee is appointed but offered less favourable terms of employment because of her sex.
- Deliberately failing or refusing to offer employment to a woman because of her sex.

8.2.2 INDIRECT DISCRIMINATION
This form of discrimination is less obvious to detect. Quite genuinely,

it might not have ever been intended by the employer. It occurs when an employer applies a requirement or condition to a woman or to a married person which they also apply to a man or an unmarried person but which is such that:

- The proportion of women or married persons who are able to comply with it is considerably smaller than the proportion of men or unmarried persons.
- The employer cannot show it to be justifiable irrespective of the sex or marital status of the applicant; and
- The condition is to the applicant's detriment because she is unable to comply with it.

In each case of indirect discrimination the key issue is whether the requirement is justifiable in considering the duties to be performed. An example would be where an employer applies a minimum height requirement of 6 foot before considering any candidate for a vacant position. More women than men are under this height and therefore unless the condition can be justified in terms of the requirements of the job itself, it would be indirectly discriminatory against women.

Where such a condition or requirement is applied by the employer and a claim of discrimination is made against them, they must show that it is objectively justified for an economic, administrative or other reason. A balance has to be struck between the discriminatory effect of the requirement or condition and the reasonable needs of the employer. The courts must ask themselves how many women will suffer as a consequence of it and how seriously will they suffer?

8.2.3 VICTIMISATION

The idea here is to prevent employees from being penalised by their employer for taking action against them under the provisions of the sex discrimination legislation. Discrimination will occur when the victimised employee is treated less favourably by the employer because they have:

- Brought, or threatened to bring, proceedings against the employer or some other relevant person.
- Given evidence or information in connection with proceedings brought by any person against the employer or other relevant person.
- Otherwise done anything under, or by reference to, the sex discrimination legislation, in relation to the employer or other relevant person.
- Alleged that the employer or other relevant person has committed an act which would contravene the sex discrimination legislation.

8.2.4 THE NEED FOR COMPARISON

A successful discrimination claim depends on a woman being able to show that she has been treated less favourably then a man because of her sex. The person with whom she compares herself can be hypothetical. Like must be compared with like, even where a hypothetical comparator is used. In defending a claim, the employer can compare a female claimant with a hypothetical man but only by reference to the same employment with the same members of staff involved. The issue of comparability can be complex. But to simplify matters the two most common areas where this issue occurs will be looked at in turn.

8.2.5 CLOTHING AND PERSONAL APPEARANCE

Discrimination can occur when the employer insists on enforcing different rules for clothing or appearance for men and women at their place of work. Most people will have conventional ideas about the way the sexes should dress, keep their hair or have earrings. These ideas will change over time.

The approach of the employment tribunal when faced with cases like these is to consider the clothing or appearance rules as a whole, rather than garment by garment. The tribunal is looking to see if the rules are more restrictive for one sex than the other. They take a pragmatic approach, men and women are different and therefore it is expected that the rules will also differ. Provided the employer enforces the rules even-handedly they are unlikely to be regarded as having discriminated against one or other sex. For example, if the rules state women must wear make-up and men must not wear beards, they are even-handed and unlikely to be seen as discriminatory provided they are enforced in equal measure.

8.2.6 PREGNANCY

In the case of a pregnant woman, the question has arisen whether comparisons with a man is possible or necessary. Pregnancy is a condition unique to women and when a pregnant woman believes she has been treated less favourably by her employer because of her condition, to search for an analogous male comparator is somewhat artificial. The comparison test in pregnancy cases is now outdated. Any woman dismissed where the primary reason can be shown to be her condition or because of absences from work due to a maternity-related illness, is entitled to claim that the dismissal is automatically unfair and that she has been discriminated against on the grounds of her sex. There is a 'protected period' which runs from conception until the end of the maternity leave period.

8.2.7 ADVERTISING

When an employer advertises a position there are rules that must be complied with to avoid discrimination. The responsibility not to discriminate will extend to the publisher of the advertisement. If there is discrimination the Equal Opportunities Commission (see Useful

Addresses) may bring an action to ensure compliance with the law. Job applicants should look out for the following signs of discrimination:

- Stereotyped words or phrases e.g. "postman" or "hostess".
- Does the job description in the advert deter women from applying?
- If there are pictures or illustrations along with the advert, do they discourage women from applying, for example, by showing only men in that working environment?
- Are there any conditions or requirements within the job specification as advertised which could be indirectly discriminatory?
- If the advert is placed in a newspaper or magazine read predominantly by one sex.

8.2.8 INTERVIEWS
Discrimination often takes place at the interview stage where:

- Male and female candidates are asked different questions.
- Questions are asked which are based on stereotypical assumptions.
- Sexist questions or remarks are made by the interviewer.
- Unnecessary questions, not relevant to the job, are asked of the interviewee in respect of domestic circumstances.

A classic example of the last point is to ask a young woman whether they have plans to start a family. If a woman feels discriminated against by the way in which the interview was handled or by the questions asked they should take the matter up with their regional Equal Opportunities Commission who will investigate the matter on their behalf (see Useful Addresses).

8.2.9 OPPORTUNITIES
Once in employment a woman can expect not to be discriminated against in the way in which the employer provides her with access to opportunities for promotion, transfer or to any other benefits or services.

8.2.10 DISMISSAL
If an employee is dismissed on the grounds of their sex or marital status this will be unlawful sex discrimination and an unfair dismissal.

8.2.11 OTHER DETRIMENT
A woman will be entitled to claim sex discrimination if she is subjected to any other detriment, other than dismissal, such as demotion, wage-cut or withdrawal of employment privileges on the grounds of her sex.

8.2.12 PENSIONS

Many employers contract out of the state pension scheme and provide benefits to their employees under a private scheme. The employer will be acting unlawfully if they do not allow equal access to the scheme for men and women. Note here that to deny part-timers access to a pension scheme will be to indirectly discriminate against women since more part-time workers are women in the UK.

8.2.13 POSITIVE DISCRIMINATION

The 1975 Act does not allow positive discrimination since that would involve deliberately appointing a woman because of her sex where candidates are equal. This approach would lead to discrimination against men and the Act is in place to protect both sexes. However, encouraging women to apply for a position is permissible by:

- Providing training for women.
- Advertising.

Such action is only permitted if the employer can show that in the preceding 12 months there have been no women or only a small proportion of women carrying out particular work.

8.2.14 GENUINE OCCUPATIONAL QUALIFICATION

If an employer can establish that being a man is a genuine occupational qualification for a job they may discriminate lawfully in certain respects. This permitted discrimination will cover advertising, interviewing, offers, refusing opportunities for promotion, training or transfers. Being a man is a genuine occupational qualification for a job in the following circumstances:

- Physiology, dramatic performance, entertainment or authenticity.
- For reasons of decency or privacy – where the job involves close physical contact or state of undress with other employees, customers or persons.
- The work is in a private home and involves close physical or social contact with, or intimate details of, a person.
- The employee lives in and only single-sex sleeping accommodation is available.
- The job is being carried out at an establishment that is single sex – e.g. a man's health clinic.
- Personal services for the welfare or education of individuals are being provided, and the recipients could identify better with a member of their own sex.
- The work is being carried out outside the UK and the laws and customs of that country prohibit a particular sex from carrying out that work.
- The work requires a married couple.

8.2.15 PART-TIMERS

Twenty-eight per cent of the workforce in the UK work part-time. Of those 88% are women. More women than men are unable to meet the requirement for full-time working. This may be to their detriment in not receiving the same employment benefits as full-timers, for example, bonuses, holiday and contractual sick pay. If this differential cannot be objectively justified by the employer it may be viewed as indirect discrimination against women if, as is usual, the part-time workforce in question is predominantly female.

With effect from July 2000 it is now unlawful to discriminate against an individual because they are a part-timer. Part-timers no longer have to rely on sex discrimination legislation to bring an action. Part-timers have new direct rights further to the European Part-time Work Directive. Under the regulations part-timers will:

- Receive the same hourly rate as comparable full-time workers.
- Receive the same hourly rate of over-time as comparable full-time workers, once they have worked more than the normal full-time hours.
- Not be excluded from training simply because they work part-time.
- Have the same entitlements to annual leave and maternity/parental leave (pro rata) as full-timers.

The new regulations apply to employees, homeworkers and agency workers.

8.2.16 SEXUAL HARASSMENT

Sexual harassment is unlawful direct discrimination. It occurs when the conduct towards a woman complainant is viewed by the victim as:

- Unwanted.
- Unreasonable.
- Offensive.

It will also include situations where the employer or member of their workforce uses such conduct as a basis for deciding on promotion, an appraisal or other employment matters. The conduct must be such that the victim felt:

- Intimidated.
- The subject of hostility.
- Humiliated.

Where a woman regards as sexual harassment conduct to which most other women would not take exception, the law states that, provided the employee has made it clear the conduct is unwelcome, any repetition may amount to harassment. Of course, many forms of conduct are objectively hostile or offensive and these do not require the employee to indicate that they are unwelcome before they may constitute harassment.

The employer has a duty to properly and thoroughly investigate an allegation of sexual harassment and to take whatever disciplinary action is appropriate against the perpetrator of the conduct. Unless the employer can show that reasonable steps were taken to prevent sexual harassment they may be held responsible for the acts of the employee. Employees who feel they are being sexually harassed at work should firstly raise a formal grievance with their employer. If this fails to address the problem adequately they may consider reporting the matter to the regional office of the Equal Opportunities Commission for further investigation (see Useful Addresses) or to a local solicitor.

8.2.17 TRANSSEXUALS AND HOMOSEXUALS

Discrimination on the grounds that a person intends to undergo, is undergoing, or has undergone gender reassignment is unlawful. There is a genuine occupational defence that is subject to the overriding requirement that the employer's actions be reasonable. The law does not currently protect job applicants or employees who are discriminated against on the grounds of sexual orientation.

8.3 ENFORCEMENT

Where sex discrimination is alleged to have occurred in the field of employment, proceedings are brought by the complainant before an employment tribunal. The complaint must be presented within 3 months from when the act was committed. To calculate the time limit, the following will be taken into consideration:

- Where the contract of employment includes a term making the contract an unlawful act, the act shall be treated as extending throughout the duration of the contract.
- Any act extending over a period shall be treated as being done at the end of that period.
- A deliberate omission by the employer shall be treated as done when the person in question decided upon it.

The tribunal may by order:

- Declare the rights of the parties.
- Make a recommendation as to a particular course of action.
- Award compensation on the same basis as the county courts award damages.

There is no limit to the amount of compensation that may be awarded by a tribunal and damages can include a sum for injury to feelings. If the employee has been dismissed and claims this was due to their sex they may also claim up to the statutory limits for unfair dismissal compensation (see Chapter 4).

8.4 THE EQUAL OPPORTUNITIES COMMISSION (EOC)

The EOC was set up specifically to work actively toward the elimination of discrimination to promote equality of opportunity between men and women generally and to keep under review the working of the Sex Discrimination Act 1975.

The EOC issues codes of practice and, if it thinks fit, is empowered to conduct a formal investigation for any purpose connected with the carrying out of its duties. In undertaking this investigation, the EOC may issue a notice requiring the production of written information or documents from the employer. It also has the power to examine witnesses. As a result, the EOC may make recommendations to the employer for changes in their procedures. The EOC may issue a non-discrimination notice during its investigations if it is satisfied that an employer has committed or is committing:

- An unlawful discriminatory act.
- A discriminatory practice.
- A breach of the provisions in respect of advertising, instructions to discriminate or pressure to discriminate.
- A breach of a term modified or included by virtue of an equality clause.

The non-discrimination notice may require the employer not to commit any such acts and to change their practices and other arrangements. If the notice is not complied with by the errant employer the EOC may apply to the county court for the issue of an injunction.

The EOC may give assistance to claimants if their case is of some complexity or raises a question of principle. Assistance will include seeking to obtain a settlement, advice and legal representation if necessary. The cost of assistance may be recovered by the EOC on an award of costs by the tribunal or from any agreed settlement (for the offices of the EOC, see Useful Addresses).

8.5 RACE DISCRIMINATION

Discrimination on racial grounds is unlawful under the Race Relations Act 1976. The provisions of that Act are very similar to those of the Sex Discrimination Act. Broadly, the Act outlaws discrimination in three ways; where it is direct, indirect or by way of victimisation. In order to determine whether a person has been discriminated against, a comparison is necessary with someone of similar ability and qualifications in similar circumstances. Like must be compared with like.

8.5.1 DIRECT DISCRIMINATION

This will occur where an employer or potential employer treats a person less favourably than he treats or would treat others on the grounds of their race.

8.5.2 INDIRECT DISCRIMINATION

An employer will discriminate indirectly if, on racial grounds, they apply to one person a requirement or condition which they apply or would apply equally to persons not of the same racial group as that person but:

- It is such that the proportion of persons in that racial group who can comply with it is considerably smaller than the proportion of persons not of that racial group who can comply with it;
- Which the employer cannot show to be justifiable irrespective of the colour, race, nationality or ethnic or national origins of the person to whom it is applied; and
- Which is to the detriment of that other person because he cannot comply with it.

An example often used to illustrate this form of discrimination would be where an employer, without good reason and unrelated to the job, demands that a job applicant has connoisseur knowledge of malt whiskey. In that case Moslems, forbidden by their religion to drink alcohol, would be indirectly discriminated against. If, however, the condition was applied because the job offered was for a whiskey-taster at a blending factory, such a requirement may not be discriminatory.

8.5.3 VICTIMISATION

This takes place where the person victimised is treated less favourably than the discriminator would treat others because the victim has:

- Brought proceedings against the discriminator or any other relevant person under the terms of the Race Relations Act.
- Given evidence or information in connection with proceedings brought by any person against the discriminator or any other person under the Act; or
- Otherwise done anything under or by reference to the Act in relation to the discriminator or any other person.
- Alleged that the discrimination or any other relevant person has committed an act which amounts to contravention of the Act.

This will also include situations where a person is victimised by the discriminator because they intend to do any of the above or the discriminator suspects they will do any of them.

8.5.4 WHAT IS RACE DISCRIMINATION?

Race discrimination, direct or indirect, takes place following less favourable treatment on racial grounds. Racial grounds covers a number of possibilities including a person's:

- Colour.
- Race.
- Nationality or national origins.
- Ethnic origin.

Clearly, nationality is quite different from race or colour and much wider in its application and would include, for example, Northern Europeans who are discriminated against on the grounds of their country of origin. Ethnic origin is added because it too can be different from a person's nationality or race. Ethnic groups can span a variety of racial or national origins and could include Sikhs or Jews. To establish an ethnic origin, the group of people must have:

- A long shared history, of which the group is conscious and which distinguishes it from other groups.
- A cultural tradition of its own including family, social customs and manners, often associated (but not necessarily) with religious observance.

The following characteristics are also relevant:

- Common geographical origin, or descent from a small number of ancestors.
- Common language (not necessarily peculiar to the group).
- Common literature.
- Common religion, different from neighbouring groups or the general community.
- Being a minority, or being in an oppressed or dominant group within a large community.

Case law has established that Sikhs, Jews and Romany gypsies comprise ethnic groups but Rastafarians do not. Interestingly, the Scots and the English have been held to be separate groups. There are many others yet to be tested.

8.5.5 DISCRIMINATION IN EMPLOYMENT

Employers are prohibited from discriminating on grounds of race at every stage of employment and at any establishment in Great Britain. Employment is given a wider definition than usual and includes employees, apprentices and contract workers. It also covers other categories of workers such as the police who are not covered under other areas of employment legislation.

8.5.6 ADVERTISEMENTS

It is unlawful for an employer to advertise a position that indicates an intention to discriminate unlawfully. It will only be lawful if there exists a genuine occupational qualification for the job (see later).

8.5.7 ENGAGEMENT

It is unlawful for an employer to discriminate on grounds of race in relation to:

- The arrangements they make for the purpose of determining who should be offered employment.
- The terms on which they offer employment.
- Refusing or deliberately omitting to offer employment.

This will cover short-listing, processing of application forms, interviewing and the offer of terms of employment itself.

8.5.8 TRAINING

No discrimination is permissible by an employer on racial grounds in the way in which the employee is afforded access to opportunities for promotion transfer or training or other employment benefits, facilities or services.

8.5.9 OTHER DETRIMENT AND DISMISSAL

Dismissal on racial grounds is almost always unfair, therefore the claim before an employment tribunal will reflect both the unfairness of the dismissal and the element of race discrimination as separate issues derived from the same facts. Subjecting an employee to any other detriment than dismissal on the ground of their race is also unlawful. Other detriments will include demotion, wage-cut etc.

8.6 EXCEPTIONS TO RACE DISCRIMINATION

The exceptions listed under this section are generally narrowly construed when tested before the courts or tribunal.

8.6.1 EMPLOYMENT OUTSIDE GREAT BRITAIN

The provisions of the Act do not apply where the employee works wholly or mainly outside Great Britain or on a British registered ship, aircraft or hovercraft, wholly outside Great Britain.

8.6.2 PRIVATE HOUSEHOLD

Except for the provisions relating to victimisation, the Act does not apply to the employment of domestic staff in a private household.

8.6.3 PUBLIC FACILITIES

Where facilities, benefits or services are being offered to the public the provisions of the Act do not apply if the employer is concerned with the provision of such benefits. For example, an employer offers a service to the public but not to an employee by virtue of a provision under the contract of employment. Provided this restriction is implemented even-handedly by the employer there will be no discrimination.

8.6.4 GENUINE OCCUPATIONAL QUALIFICATION

Discrimination will be lawful by an employer where the arrangements they make for selection are further to a genuine occupational qualification for the job. The requirement by an employer that an employee must belong to a particular racial group is justified only where:

- The job involves participation in a dramatic performance or other entertainment in a capacity for which a person of that racial group is required for reasons of authenticity.
- Physiology requires a particular colour or race (e.g. an artist's model).
- In a public restaurant or bar, where authenticity requires members from a particular racial group (e.g. Chinese staff in a Chinese restaurant).
- In the provision of personal welfare services to a particular racial group, where it would be better provided by someone of the same racial group (e.g. in a group promoting the welfare of Afro-Caribbean mothers, the work may be carried out more effectively by someone of the same Afro-Caribbean origin).

8.6.5 ACTS DONE UNDER STATUTORY AUTHORITY

No race discrimination will occur if the employer acts in accordance with any condition required by law.

8.6.6 POSITIVE DISCRIMINATION

Positive discrimination which favours people of a particular racial group, to provide access to training and work is permissible provided that if at any time within the preceding 12 months:

- There were no people from that group doing work at that establishment.
- The proportion of people from that group doing work at that establishment is small in comparison with:

1. All other staff employed.
2. The population of the area from which the employer normally recruits their workforce.

8.7 RACIAL HARASSMENT

Racial harassment of an individual can amount to race discrimination but it attracts fewer cases then its counterpart sexual harassment. The harassment may be verbal, non-verbal or physical. Such activity must amount to a detriment. For example, for security guards to search every black entrant into premises and not every white could be regarded as harassment. Insults may also amount to harassment but only where it can be shown that the employee has been in some way disadvantaged by the language used. The fact that distress has been caused will not in itself be enough for it to be an unlawful act.

In a recently decided case it was held that it was racial harassment based on a person's national origins where the employer failed to prevent colleagues subjecting the employee to Irish jokes and comments.

8.8 ENFORCEMENT

An individual who wishes to complain that they have been discriminated against on racial grounds may present their claim to an employment tribunal. The complaint must be brought within 3 months from the time that the act complained of was done. The tribunal may consider a complaint made outside this time limit if it is just and equitable to do so in the circumstances of the case. In calculating the time limit the following points may be of assistance:

- Where the inclusion of a term into a contract of employment renders the making of the contract an unlawful act, the act shall be treated as extending throughout the duration of the contract.
- Any act extending over a period shall be regarded as having been done at the end of that period.
- A deliberate omission shall be regarded as having been done when the person in question decided upon it.
- In the case of a single act, the time will run when the course of action is complete.

Regarding the last point, if the act is continuing against the employee, the time limit is continually refreshed and on-going.

8.9 COMMISSION FOR RACIAL EQUALITY (CRE)

The 1976 Act established a Commission for Racial Equality whose function is to work towards the elimination of discrimination, the promotion of equality of opportunity, good race relations and monitoring the working of the Act. Where an employee or job applicant believes they have been subjected to race discrimination, they may make contact with their regional CRE office who are empowered to assist with the investigation of their complaint (see Useful Addresses). The CRE also issues codes of practice.

8.9.1 THE COMMISSION FOR RACIAL EQUALITY AND NON-DISCRIMINATION NOTICES

In addition to undertaking investigations, on request, against employers who are allegedly acting in a discriminatory fashion, the CRE in the course of their enquiries may serve a non-discrimination notice on the employer, requiring them:

- Not to commit such acts.
- To change certain practices or arrangements.

To do this the CRE must first be satisfied that the employer is committing, or has committed, an unlawful discriminatory act or practice or is guilty of placing or publishing an unlawful discriminatory advertisement or has applied pressure to discriminate unlawfully.

The CRE may require verification from the employer that they have complied with the notice. This must be supplied to the CRE within a specified period of time and not later than 5 years from the date the notice became final.

As can be seen, the CRE have a wide range of powers to prevent or curtail race discrimination at the workplace. Employees who believe they have a valid complaint should not hesitate to contact the CRE whose subsequent process of investigation is taken seriously by most employers (see Useful Addresses). Local Employment offices and Job Centres are also a useful source of primary information.

8.10 REMEDIES

8.10.1 DECLARATORY ORDER
The tribunal may issue an order declaring the rights of the complainant and the respondent in relation to the act about which a complaint has been made.

8.10.2 RECOMMENDING REMEDIAL ACTION
The tribunal may recommend that an employer, within a specified period of time, takes some form of practical action to avoid or reduce the adverse effect presently experienced by the complainant.

8.10.3 COMPENSATION
A monetary award can be made if the complainant has suffered loss and this will include injury to feelings and compensation for loss of opportunity in the labour market. There is no ceiling to the amount of compensation that may be awarded.

8.11 DISABLED EMPLOYEES
The Disability Discrimination Act 1995, has as its central objective, the elimination of discrimination against disabled people particularly at their place of work.

8.11.1 THE MEANING OF DISABILITY
Under the provisions a person is regarded as having a disability if they have a physical or mental impairment which has a substantial and long-term adverse effect on their ability to carry out normal day-to-day activities. The constituent parts of this definition can be assessed in more detail.

Impairment
Mental impairment includes an impairment resulting from or consisting of a mental illness only if it is a clinically well-recognised

illness, for example mentioned in the World Health Organisation's International Classification of Diseases.

Long-term Effect

A long-term effect is defined as one that has lasted at least 12 months or the period for which it lasts can reasonably be expected to be at least 12 months. Of course, this prediction must be supported by an appropriate medical report.

Day-to-day Activities

The impairment must affect normal day-to-day activities. This will be deemed to have occurred when the impairment affects one or more of the following:

- Mobility.
- Manual dexterity.
- Physical co-ordination.
- Continence.
- Ability to lift.
- Ability to carry or otherwise move everyday objects.
- Speech.
- Hearing.
- Eyesight.
- Memory.
- Ability to concentrate or learn.
- Ability to perceive physical danger.
- Substantial and adverse effect.

In determining whether an impairment has an adverse effect on a person's ability to carry out activities, the fact that a person can, with difficulty and great effort, carry out the activities does not mean that their ability to carry them out has not been impaired. In addition, where the person is on medication, consideration must be given to how the activities would have been affected without medication. Substantial means more than 'minor' or 'trivial'. In general, asthma, epilepsy, ME, post-traumatic stress disorder, ureteric colic and depression being treated by Prozac have all been held by tribunals to be disability within the meaning of the Act.

8.11.2 DISCRIMINATION IN EMPLOYMENT

It is unlawful for an employer to discriminate against a disabled person in the arrangements made for determining to whom he should offer employment, the terms upon which employment is offered, refusal to offer, or deliberately not offering, employment. In much the same way that the race and sex discrimination laws operate, it is also unlawful to discriminate against a disabled person in the terms and conditions, opportunities for promotion, transfers and training provided by the employer. Disabled employees must not be dismissed on the ground of their disability or subjected to any other detriment.

8.11.3 TREATED LESS FAVOURABLY

Less favourable treatment of an employee will be discriminatory unless the employer can justify the treatment. There are 4 specified conditions in which justification can be established as reasonable in the circumstances:

1. The disabled person is unsuitable for the employment.
2. The disabled person is less suitable for the employment than another applicant who was appointed.
3. The nature of the disabled person's disability significantly impedes, or would significantly impede, the performance of their duties.
4. The nature of the disabled person's disability would significantly reduce the value of any training provided by the employer.

Closely linked to less favourable treatment is the employer's duty to take such steps as are reasonable to prevent any work arrangements or any physical features of the employer's premises from placing a disabled applicant or employee at a substantial disadvantage compared to non-disabled applicants or employee (see section 8.11.4). If an employer has not complied with his duty to make adjustments, the defence of justification is only available if the less favourable   treatment would have been justified even if the duty had been complied with.

8.11.4 DUTY TO MAKE REASONABLE ADJUSTMENTS

In certain circumstances a specific duty is placed on the employer, in law, to make changes to work arrangements or to any physical feature of the work premises which places the disabled person at a substantial disadvantage in comparison with able-bodied persons. The duty on the employer is to take all reasonable steps in the circumstances to alter the arrangements or physical feature or to prevent them from having that effect.

The disabled person may be either an applicant or present employee. If a conclusion may be drawn that an arrangement or a physical feature does treat the disabled person less favourably, the employer, to defend their position, must then show that to alter the arrangements or physical feature would be unreasonable in all the circumstances.

An employee may therefore expect an employer, or prospective employer, to make reasonable adjustments to the workplace in order to overcome the practical effects of the disability. That does not mean the employer is under a duty to make the best adjustment possible in the circumstances but to do what may be reasonably expected. Reasonable adjustments may include:

* Widening doorways or making other adjustments to premises.
* Re-allocating some of the disabled person's duties.

- Transferring them to fill an existing vacancy.
- Altering their hours of work.
- Assigning them to a different place of work, or allowing them to work from home.
- Allowing them to be absent during working hours for assessment or treatment.
- Providing training.
- Acquiring or modifying equipment.
- Modifying instructions or manuals.
- Providing a reader.
- Providing supervision.
- Modifying testing and assessment procedures.

In determining what steps it is reasonable for an employee to take, the following will be relevant:

- Is it practicable for the employer to take the steps?
- What are the costs?
- What are the employer's resources?
- Is any financial or other assistance available to the employer?

In addition, there is no general duty on an employer to require them to adapt their workplace or change their working practices to make them accessible in anticipation of possibly having a disabled applicant or employee at some time in the future.

8.11.5 SMALL EMPLOYERS

Where the employer employs fewer than 15 staff they are exempt from claims of disability discrimination. However, they are encouraged to follow good practice guidelines.

8.11.6 BRINGING A CLAIM

The disabled employee who believes they have been discriminated against by their employer or prospective employer may bring an action for compensation before an employment tribunal. The tribunal's powers are similar to those that apply to complaints of race and sex discrimination. There is no upper limit to compensation. In addition, an amount may be awarded for injury to feelings.

The National Disability Council and the Northern Ireland Disability Council established under the Act are responsible for drawing up codes of practice which effect disabled people in the workplace.

8.11.7 THE DISABILITY RIGHTS COMMISSION

The Disability Rights Commission (DRC) has statutory powers of enforcement that are available to the EOC and the CRE. The DRC'S mission is to work towards the elimination of discrimination against disabled people. It also promotes the equalisation of opportunities for disabled people with those of non-disabled people, promote good practice among employers and service providers, advise the Government on law about discrimination against disabled people and be a central source of advice for employers and business.

8.12 CASE STUDY

Anthony applies for a job with Gossip Radio FM. Gossip Radio have 36 employees. He is interviewed by Kelvin McDifficult. Anthony is blind, and has been so since birth. He is applying for a job as a receptionist. At the interview Kelvin says that although he does not have anything against taking on a blind person, the receptionist's console, as it stands, can only be operated by a sighted operator. In addition, Kelvin says he is allergic to Golden Labradors such as Anna, Anthony's faithful guide dog. One week later Anthony receives a letter from Kelvin saying his application for the position was unsuccessful. Anthony seeks legal advice.

Gossip Radio has more than 15 employees and, therefore, the provisions of the Disability Discrimination Act apply to it. Upon investigation, which Kelvin McDifficult was not prepared to undertake because he was busy and did not have the time, it was discovered that the receptionist's console could be adapted for use by a blind person for the small cost of £250.00. Anthony files a claim of disability discrimination against Gossip Radio and is successful. The tribunal found that Gossip Radio should have undertaken the 'reasonable adjustment' to their reception console since Anthony (on all other criteria) was the best candidate for the job. Anthony is awarded £16,000 compensation to cover his losses and injury to feelings. Kelvin's alleged allergy to Golden Labradors is ruled as irrelevant.

TRADE UNION MEMBERSHIP

9.1 EMPLOYMENT PROTECTION

Apart from the right not to be unfairly dismissed or victimised on the grounds of membership or non-membership of a trade union (as detailed in Section 4.4), the law provides a number of other safeguards intended to prevent bias against an individual on the same grounds.

9.2 UNION MEMBERSHIP RIGHTS

Any employee who is a member of a trade union is entitled:

- Not to be refused employment because of their membership.
- Not to be dismissed on the grounds of membership or for taking part in trade union activities – such dismissals will be classed as automatically unfair (this includes dismissal on grounds related to recognition or de-recognition and no qualifying period of employment applies).
- Not to be subjected to action short of dismissal by their employer for reasons of membership or for taking part in trade union activities.
- To reasonable time off work to take part in trade union activities (trade union officials being entitled to paid time off for the same).
- Not to suffer unauthorised or excessive deductions from wages by reason of union subscriptions.
- Not to be discriminated against on grounds of trade union membership, whether that discrimination consists of an act or failure to act.
- Not to be 'blacklisted' in connection with trade union activities by an employer or agency for recruitment purposes.
- Not to be selected for redundancy on grounds relating to membership, taking part in trade union activities or to recognition or de-recognition (no qualifying period of employment applies).

9.3 UNION NON-MEMBERSHIP RIGHTS

Until as recently as 1991 it was lawful for an employer only to offer work to employees who were members of a particular trade union. This practice was known as the 'closed shop'. It is now unlawful to refuse to recruit an individual because they are not a member of a particular, or any, trade union.

'Refusal' is defined as a deliberate omission to deal with a person's application, to cause its withdrawal or to offer the position with such unreasonable attached terms that it acts as a deliberate disincentive to non-union applicants. Refusal of employment will be deemed to have been on union non-membership grounds and unlawful where:

- A published advertisement indicates employment is available only for union members.
- A published advertisement contains a requirement which a non-union member would be unwilling to accept.
- There exists an arrangement or practice that puts forward applicants for consideration who are approved by the union and are members of a particular union.

9.4 REMEDIES

Where a person believes they have been refused employment on the grounds of non-membership or membership of a trade union, they have the right to take the matter before an employment tribunal. The complaint must be presented within 3 months of the refusal or other conduct complained of unless there exists a reason why it was not reasonably practicable to do so. Where the employer has acted under pressure from a trade union to so act against non-members the union may face the same proceedings brought against the employer.

If the complaint is upheld by the tribunal, there will be a declaration to that effect. If it is fair to do so in the circumstances, the employer (and union if joined) may be ordered to pay compensation to the individual including an amount in respect of injury to feelings. The maximum award is £50,000.

The tribunal also has the power to order the employer to take action, within a specified period of time, to reduce or avoid the same situation in the future. If the employer fails, without reasonable justification, a further award may be made.

9.5 UNION MEMBERS RIGHTS IN RESPECT OF THEIR UNION

Every trade union member, including those who wish to be members of a particular union, have the following rights in relation to their union:

- Not to be excluded or expelled except on certain grounds and in accordance with union rules.
- To terminate trade union membership by giving reasonable notice and complying with reasonable conditions.
- Not to have unjustifiable disciplinary action taken against them by the trade union.
- To be balloted before industrial action.
- To inspect the union's accounts.
- To apply for a remedy to the High Court where the trustees of the union's property act unlawfully.

9.5.1 EXCLUSION OR EXPULSION FROM UNION MEMBERSHIP

The general right not to be excluded or expelled from any union unless it is permitted by statute gives employees considerable freedom to join their first choice of union when more than one union organises employees of a similar type. The permitted reasons for exclusion or expulsion are as follows:

- Where the union's rules restrict membership to workers employed in a specified trade or industry, or to workers of a particular occupational description, or who hold specified qualifications or experience.
- Where the union only operates in certain parts of Great Britain and the individual being outside those parts does not therefore qualify for membership.
- Where the union only operates with one employer or group of employers and the individual is not employed by that employer.
- The individual's conduct.

Should an employee feel that they have been excluded or expelled outside of the above reasons, they may apply to an employment tribunal for a declaration that their rights have been breached. The complaint to the employment tribunal against the union must be presented within 6 months from the refusal or expulsion. This will only be extended if the complainant can show that it was not reasonably practicable to bring the complaint at an earlier opportunity.

Where a declaration is made stating that the rights have been breached, the complainant will be entitled to compensation. The individual cannot apply for compensation until 4 weeks after the date of the declaration. This 4 week period is designed to allow the trade union to admit or readmit the complainant to their membership. Application for compensation must be made within 6 months of the declaration. For the amounts of compensation available see generally Chapter 4.

9.5.2 UNJUSTIFIABLE DISCIPLINE

Trade union members can expect to be dealt with in accordance with the union rules and natural justice. Should there be a breach of either, the member may apply to the High Court for an injunction to prevent the disciplinary action from continuing and a declaration of their rights. In addition to these common law rights, the trade union member has a statutory right not to be unjustifiably disciplined by a union. This right is conferred over and above any contractual or membership right. There exist 12 categories of conduct for which it will be regarded as unjustifiable, if a member is disciplined by the union. They are:

- Failing to participate in or support, or oppose, any industrial action.
- Failing to breach a contract of employment or other agreement with the employer for the purposes of industrial action.
- Asserting that the union or any of its officials is in breach of its obligations in law.

- Encouraging or assisting another person to fulfil obligations to the employer.
- Failing to comply with any requirement imposed as a result of unjustifiable disciplinary action taken against themselves or another.
- Failing to agree to the deduction of union dues from wages.
- Resigning or proposing to resign from the union or another union, or being or becoming, or proposing or refusing to become, a member of another union.
- Working or proposing to work with individuals who do not belong to a particular union.
- Working or proposing to work for an employer of such individuals.
- Requiring the union to do an act that certain statutory provisions require it to do on a member's demand.
- Consulting or requesting assistance from the Certification Officer or other similar persons.
- Proposing or preparing to do any of the above.

Disciplinary action is defined as including expulsion from the union, fines and the withholding of benefits normally provided by the union or subjection to any other detriment. Where the union member believes they have a complaint of unjustifiable discipline it must be brought before an employment tribunal within 3 months of the act complained of. An extension of time is possible if the complaint was not reasonably practicable within this limitation.

If the complaint is well-founded, a declaration to that effect will be made by the tribunal. Compensation may then be ordered by the tribunal if the union has reversed its disciplinary measures or by the Employment Appeal Tribunal if it has not. Applications must be made not earlier than 4 weeks and not later than 6 months after the disciplinary action is declared unjustifiable.

9.5.3 RIGHT TO BE BALLOTED

Should a union authorise or endorse industrial action in breach of statutory balloting procedure, individual union members may, by right, seek a court order requiring the union to withdraw its authorisation.

9.5.4 RIGHT TO TERMINATE UNION MEMBERSHIP

This statutory right implies into every contract of employment a term conferring a right on the union member to terminate their membership upon serving the union reasonable notice and by complying with any reasonable union conditions.

9.5.5 TRADE UNION FINANCIAL INFORMATION

Union members are entitled to an annual written statement on the union's finances including details of the auditor's report. The statement must explain the steps a member can take if they are concerned about financial irregularities in the conduct of the union's affairs. In most cases the union will comply with this requirement by publishing the required statement in the union's journal.

9.6 UNION SUBSCRIPTION – DEDUCTION FROM WAGES

A union is required by law to ballot its members in respect of political objectives. Ballots must be held to introduce funds for political objectives and to retain them. Furthermore, a political fund must be administered separately by the union from their other general funds and only money in the political fund may be used for political purposes.

Where a union has such a political fund, the members of that union are entitled to 'contract-out' of that portion of the member's subscriptions which is set aside to be paid into the political fund. This portion of the subscription is known as the 'political levy'. Any employer who operates a 'check-off' system must stop deducting the political levy element of the union subscription at the request of a member and employee to contract-out.

Deductions may only be made in accordance with an authorisation signed and dated by the employee. Authorisations are now treated as of unlimited duration until withdrawal. No advance notice of any increase in the amount deducted is required. Where an employer makes a deduction in contravention of the above provisions, the employee may complain to an employment tribunal within 3 months from the last relevant deduction. This period may be extended if grounds exist to show why an earlier complaint was not reasonably practicable. The tribunal may order repayment of the amount improperly deducted.

9.7 ACTION SHORT OF DISMISSAL

It is unlawful for an employer to take adverse action short of dismissal against an employee on grounds relating to recognition or de-recognition of a union (see section 9.11). All employees are entitled not to have action taken against them as individuals by their employer that acts to:

- Prevent, penalise or deter them from being or seeking to become members of an independent trade union.
- To prevent, penalise or deter them from taking part in the activities of an independent trade union.
- To compel them to join any trade union.
- To force them to make payments to some other body in the event of their failure to become or cease to become a member of an independent trade union.

An employee who complains of such action being taken against them has the right to take the matter to an employment tribunal. The employer will then be requested to explain why such action was taken and that its purpose was not to contravene the employee's rights. The complaint must be brought within 3 months of the act complained of, or where that is shown not to have been reasonably practicable, the tribunal at their discretion may extend the limitation period. If the complaint is shown to be well-founded, the tribunal is empowered to award such an amount in favour of the employee as it considers fair in the circumstances. The tribunal will consider the nature of the right infringed by the employer's actions and any losses the employee may have suffered as a consequence.

9.8 DISMISSAL OF STRIKING EMPLOYEES

The dismissal of an employee for participating in official industrial action will be automatically unfair if it occurs during the first 8 weeks of such participation. A dismissal will also be unfair after that period if the employer has failed to take reasonable procedural steps to resolve the dispute. There is no qualifying period of employment and no age limit for employees to take advantage of this provision. In addition, any selection for redundancy on the basis that the employee has taken part in official industrial action is also unfair. Unfairly dismissed strikers will be entitled to reinstatement only after a strike is over.

There is no equivalent protection for employees participating in unofficial industrial action.

9.9 TIME OFF FOR TRADE UNION ACTIVITIES

A trade union member is entitled in law, where the employer recognises the union in question, to time off during working hours to take part in union activities. The permissible activities are defined as:

- Any activities of the trade union of which the employee is a member.
- Any activities where the employee is acting as a representative of the union.

These activities do not include those which are themselves industrial action and the time off in order to participate is without pay. These activities will include:

- Attending workplace meetings to discuss and vote on the outcome of negotiations with the employer.
- Discussing workplace issues with full-time union officials.
- Voting, in properly conducted ballots, on industrial action and union elections.

9.9.1 TRADE UNION OFFICIALS AND TIME OFF

Employers must allow employees who are trade union officials of a recognised union, time off from work with pay in order to carry out industrial relations duties and to undertake necessary training. An 'official' is a trade union member that has been appointed or elected in accordance with the union's rules. ACAS has issued a Code of Practice relevant to union officials and the circumstances in which the employer should allow paid time off to fulfil union duties. Appropriate matters for which time off should be granted are listed as:

- Terms and Conditions of employment – including working environment, pay, holidays, pensions, use of employer's machinery and plant etc.
- Engagement or non-engagement, termination or suspension of employment or the duties of employment, of one or more workers – including human resource planning, redundancy and dismissal arrangements etc.
- Allocation of work or the duties of employment as between workers or groups of workers – including job grading, flexible working practices etc.
- Matters of discipline – including procedures, representation, appeals etc.
- Trade union membership or non-membership – including representational arrangements, union involvement etc.
- Facilities for officials of trade unions – including accommodation, equipment etc.
- Machinery for negotiation or consultation and other procedures - including arrangements for collective bargaining, joint consultation, communication with members, officials and the employer etc.

In addition, the Code suggests reasonable time off should be granted to allow officials to prepare for negotiations, inform members of progress, explain outcomes to members and to prepare meetings with employers where the trade union has only representational rights.

9.10 COLLECTIVE AGREEMENTS AND THE INDIVIDUAL'S CONTRACT OF EMPLOYMENT

Large industries and employers often, by choice or otherwise, decide on the terms and conditions of employment of workers within their industry or with that employer, by collective agreement. That is, instead of each worker individually negotiating their contract terms or any subsequent amendment (e.g. wage rise) with their employer, these negotiations are done collectively on behalf of the employees by a recognised trade union. It is reckoned that in the UK some 50% of the workforce are subject to collective agreements.

In practice, these collective agreements form the basis for many workers contract of employment. Collective agreements are permissible in relation to any or all of the following matters:

- Terms and conditions of employment, including the physical working environment.
- Engagement or non-engagement, or the duties of employment, of one or more workers.

- Allocation of work.
- Discipline.
- Membership or non-membership of a trade union.
- Facilities available to trade union officials.
- Machinery for negotiation, consultation and union recognition.

In order to be legally enforceable, the collective agreement must be in writing and expressly state that the parties intend the agreement to be a legally enforceable contract. In effect, most collective agreements are not legally enforceable against the employer, but are regarded as binding in honour only.

9.10.1 EFFECT ON THE INDIVIDUAL CONTRACT OF EMPLOYMENT

Even where the nature of the collective agreement is not intended to be legally binding between the union and the employer, the terms and conditions negotiated further to the agreement may become legally binding as they take effect through incorporation into the employee's contract of employment. For example, there would be a breach of each employee's individual contract of employment if the employer suddenly stops paying an increased amount where there exists a collectively agreed wage rise that has been paid by the employer for a period of time. This would allow the employee to take legal proceedings for damages directly against their employer. This incorporation can occur by express reference or impliedly through custom and practice.

Should there be a change of employer following the transfer of a business, there exists statutory provisions which ensure the transference of any existing collective agreement to the new employer.

9.10.2 INDIVIDUALISED CONTRACTS

Where employees are covered by collectively negotiated terms and conditions of employment, they are entitled to seek redress if they are dismissed or suffer some other detriment for refusing to accept an individualised contract (which contains terms different from those contained in a collective agreement) from their employer. Employers and employees are still be free to agree individual contracts even where a union is recognised and there is a collective agreement in force.

9.11 COMPULSORY TRADE UNION RECOGNITION AND DE-RECOGNITION

There is now a new statutory right of recognition for trade unions where the relevant workforce shows its support by a majority joining the union or voting in favour of recognition in a ballot. Applications for recognition and de-recognition are dealt with by a Central Arbitration Committee. The provisions are intended to apply when unions and employers are unable to reach agreement voluntarily.

In order to trigger the statutory procedure, the trade union (or two or more unions acting jointly) must first make a written application requesting recognition to the employer. The trade union must have a certificate of independence and the employer and any associated employers must employ at least 21 workers on the day the request is made, or employ an average of at least 21 workers in the 13 week period ending with that day. The recognition procedures therefore do not apply to employers who employ 20 or fewer employees.

The employer then has ten working days after receipt of the written request to agree with the union that it is to be recognised as entitled to conduct collective bargaining on behalf of a 'bargaining unit' i.e. the group of workers concerned. If agreement is reached, that is the end of the statutory procedure. However, if the employer informs the union that he does not accept the request but is still happy to negotiate, negotiations may continue for a further period of 20 working days (or a longer period with agreement). ACAS are available to provide help in the conduct of negotiations.

If the employer rejects the request either during the initial period or during the extended negotiation period, the trade union may apply to the Central Arbitration Committee (CAC) for a written decision on the appropriate bargaining unit and whether a majority of the workers support recognition.

The CAC may not proceed with an application unless it decides that:

- At least 10% of the workers in the proposed bargaining unit are union members; and
- There is evidence that a majority of the workers in the proposed bargaining unit would be likely to favour recognition.

If a majority of the workers in the bargaining unit are already union members, the CAC may issue a declaration that the union is recognised without the need for a ballot ("automatic recognition"), unless one of the conditions set out below applies:

- The CAC is satisfied that a ballot should be held in the interests of good industrial relations.
- A significant number of the union members inform the CAC that they do not want the union to conduct collective bargaining on their behalf; or
- Membership evidence is produced which casts doubt as to whether a significant number of the union members in the bargaining unit want the union to conduct collective bargaining on their behalf.

Where a majority of the workers in the bargaining unit are not union members or where one of the conditions above applies, the CAC should then arrange for the holding of a secret ballot in which the workers are asked to vote on whether they want the union to be recognised. The ballot must be conducted by an independent scrutineer appointed by the CAC within 20 working days of his appointment. It can be either a workplace or a postal ballot. The costs of the ballot are split equally between the employer and the union. The CAC must then issue a declaration that the union is recognised, if the result of the ballot is that the union is supported by:

- A majority of the workers voting; and
- At least 40% of the workers in the bargaining unit who are eligible to vote.

Once a union is recognised, the parties will be left to agree arrangements by which they will conduct collective bargaining. The CAC will assist or intervene if no agreement can be reached. The CAC has the power to impose a procedure where the parties fail to reach agreement and this will be legally binding. That procedure will be limited to pay, hours and holidays. Once the CAC has imposed a procedure, the parties can vary it by written agreement.

Employers are also obliged to inform and consult unions recognised under the statutory procedure on their training policies and plans on a six-monthly basis where the CAC has specified a method of collective bargaining.

9.11.1 DE-RECOGNITION

Both the employer and/or the workers may apply to the CAC for de-recognition. There are a number of different de-recognition procedures. These are:

- Procedures for the employer to end statutory recognition on the ground that the number of workers employed has fallen below 21.
- Procedures for the employer or the workers to end statutory recognition on the ground that there is now only minority support for the union within the bargaining unit.
- Procedures for the employer to end "automatic" statutory recognition on the grounds that less than half of the workers in the bargaining unit now belong to the union and there is now only minority support for the union within the bargaining unit.
- Procedures for the workers to end voluntary recognition of a non-independent union on the ground that there is only minority support for the union within the bargaining unit.

Except in the latter case, applications for de-recognition may only be accepted three or more years after the date of a CAC declaration. In the latter case, de-recognition procedures may be invoked at any time. The de-recognition procedures are similar to those for recognition.

9.12 CASE STUDY

Edward runs a small family catering business called 'Fruitcake Fancy'. He believes employees should do what they are told and be grateful for the work and money he pays them. Jennifer joined Edward 6 months ago from university and is appalled at Edward's dictatorial manner towards his staff. Jennifer joins a union for protection in case Edward should make unreasonable demands of her at work.

Edward finds out about Jennifer's union membership and is incensed at what he regards as disloyalty to the family business. Edward is aware that to dismiss Jennifer for her union affiliation is highly likely to succeed in an unfair dismissal claim. He does not dismiss Jennifer but he refuses to fund any training over the next 6 months (such training is expected within the industry) and when her supervisor leaves he refuses to consider Jennifer for promotion. Jennifer seeks legal advice.

Although Edward's behaviour has been subtle, he has acted in a manner that penalises Jennifer for being a member of an independent trade union and he has acted unlawfully. Jennifer is advised to take her complaint to an employment tribunal and does so. The tribunal find Jennifer has suffered 'action short of dismissal' and has been discriminated against unlawfully for her trade union membership. The tribunal awards Jennifer £4,000, refusing to accept Edward's explanations in respect of his behaviour towards her. The award would have been considerably higher had Jennifer left Edward's employment as a result of his misconduct.

CHAPTER TEN

MATERNITY AND PARENTAL LEAVE

10.1 INTRODUCTION

There are many rights which currently exist in the UK specifically to protect pregnant women, to provide a period of leave for the mother immediately before and after the birth of their child and to allow them to return to their place of work. The statutory rights in relation to maternity are broadly the following:

- Time off for antenatal care with pay.
- The right not to be unfairly dismissed or suffer any other detriment for a reason connected to maternity.
- Maternity pay.
- The right, in certain circumstances, to return to work after confinement.

As with most employment rights, some exclusions exist for pregnant women. These are:

- Members of the police force.
- Women engaged in share fishing.
- Self-employed.

10.2 MATERNITY RIGHTS DURING PREGNANCY

Any pregnant woman who has, on the advice of their doctor, health visitor or midwife, made an appointment for ante-natal care has the right to reasonable time off during working hours to enable them to undertake the appointment. They are entitled to be paid for their absence at the normal hourly rate.

- No employer must unreasonably refuse time off for ante-natal care.
- Time off for ante-natal care must be paid.
- Ante-natal care includes medical examinations, parent craft and relaxation classes.
- There is no minimum service or working hours per week requirement before the woman may enjoy these rights.

In return for these rights the employee is expected to act reasonably and except for the first appointment for ante-natal care she must, if requested by the employer, produce for inspection:

- A certificate from her doctor, midwife or health visitor stating that she is pregnant.
- An appointment card.

The employee should be paid her normal hourly rate of pay during her time off for ante-natal care. This rate is calculated by dividing the amount of a week's pay by the number of normal working hours in a week. The normal working hours will usually be clearly stated in a contract of employment, letter of appointment or written statement of particulars of employment. If the hours are variable, an average should be taken over the preceding 12 working weeks. If 12 weeks have not been worked the hours should be reasonably estimated by reference to custom and practice. Overtime is only counted if the employee is contractually obliged to work additional hours as the needs of the business dictates.

10.3 REMEDIES

A woman who believes she has been unreasonably refused time off for ante-natal care may complain to an employment tribunal within 3 months from the date of the appointment concerned. This may be extended if there are practical reasons why a complaint within this time period was not possible. If the complaint is upheld, the tribunal will make a declaration to that effect and order payment of the money due.

10.4 DISMISSAL FOR REQUESTING OR ASSERTING THE RIGHT TO TIME OFF

Any employee who is dismissed for seeking to assert, or asserting, the right to time off for ante-natal care will have been dismissed unlawfully. An ensuing claim for unfair dismissal may be brought before an employment tribunal. There is no service requirement.

10.5 PREGNANCY – PROTECTION FROM DISMISSAL

Regardless of length of service or weekly hours, it is automatically unfair to dismiss a woman if the reason or principal reason is the following:

- That she is pregnant.
- Any reason connected with her pregnancy.
- Any reason connected with her having given birth to a child.
- Because she took advantage of the benefits of maternity leave.
- That, because of her pregnancy, she was selected for redundancy in preference to other comparable employees.

A dismissal in connection with pregnancy may also amount to sex discrimination (see Chapter 8). A woman also has the right not to be subjected to any detriment for reasons relating to pregnancy, childbirth or maternity.

10.6 EXCEPTIONS

- Where the employee is dismissed with due notice because her pregnancy-related incapacity or because her continued employment would lead to a breach of the law (usually on grounds of health and safety) she will not be entitled to claim unfair dismissal.

- Any dismissal which is on grounds largely or wholly unrelated to pregnancy or childbirth. For example, a genuinely co-incidental redundancy situation.

10.7 WRITTEN STATEMENT OF REASONS FOR DISMISSAL

Normally an employee requires 1 years' continuous service before being entitled to a written statement of the reasons for dismissal. However if the employee is dismissed during pregnancy or statutory maternity leave, irrespective of her length of service, the following will apply:

- She will be entitled to an accurate written statement of the reasons.
- She need not formally request this statement.

If the employer fails to provide a statement or it is unsatisfactory or allegedly untrue, the employee may complain to an employment tribunal within 3 months of the refusal or receipt of the inadequate reasons.

10.8 REMEDIES

Any claim for automatic unfair dismissal for a principal reason connected with pregnancy or childbirth may be brought before an employment tribunal within 3 months of the dismissal.

10.9 MATERNITY LEAVE AND THE RIGHT TO RETURN TO WORK

Rather confusingly there are potentially three situations where the employee has the right to return to work within a specified period of time. Two are statutory, one is contractual. The legislation no longer refers to a right to return. Instead, it refers to a right to take either ordinary maternity leave or additional maternity leave. The three situations are as follows:

1. The right to 18 weeks ordinary maternity leave.
2. The right to additional maternity leave beginning at the end of ordinary maternity leave and continuing until the end of the period of 29 weeks beginning with the actual week of childbirth.
3. The right to any greater period of maternity leave/absence within the contract of employment or as otherwise agreed between the employer and employee.

10.10 ORDINARY MATERNITY LEAVE PERIOD

All pregnant employees are entitled to at least 18 weeks statutory maternity leave. This applies regardless of their length of service or hours of work.

10.10.1 COMMENCEMENT

The 18 weeks leave may commence at any time after the beginning of the 11th week before the expected week of confinement (EWC). The basic 18 week leave provision will be triggered if on the first day after the beginning of the 6th week before the EWC the employee has:

- Given a notified leave date after the 6th week before the EWC.
- Is absent due to a pregnancy-related illness.

Leave will commence on the actual date of birth if earlier than the notified leave date. It follows that the basic 18 weeks leave can commence in 1 of 3 ways:

1. By childbirth itself.
2. Pregnancy-related illness any time after the 6th week before the expected week of childbirth.
3. By the employee giving 21 days notice to the employer of the date on which she wishes to commence her maternity leave.

In return for the benefit of the 18 weeks leave the employee must comply with certain procedural requirements to be fair to the employer. She must:

- Tell the employer that she is pregnant – in practice at the earliest opportunity.
- Notify the employer of her expected week of childbirth by way of appropriate medical certificate.
- Provide notification of the date when she wishes leave to commence.
- Give notification to the employer:

1. Not later than 21 days before she intends to commence leave.
2. As soon as reasonably practicable if the 21 days notice provision cannot be complied with for good reason.

Written notice of pregnancy is not essential. Notification of the date of commencement of maternity leave need not be given in writing unless the employer requests written notification.

10.10.2 EARLY RETURN
This is possible if the employee provides the employer with at least 21 days notice of her intended early return date.

10.10.3 RETURN ON THE DUE DATE
An employee need not give notice of return if she intends to return at the end of her ordinary maternity leave period. She can simply present herself for work.

10.10.4 EXTENSION
This may occur in the following situations:

- The baby is overdue, in which case the 18 week period is extended to the date of the birth plus a minimum of 2 weeks, since it is unlawful for a woman to return to work less than two weeks after childbirth.
- Where health and safety reasons prohibit the mother from returning

which are related to the recent birth of the child or breast feeding. Where this occurs the period of 18 weeks will be extended until it is safe for her to return.

Sickness at the end of maternity leave will not postpone return. Instead, normal sick leave procedures at the woman's place of work will apply. A woman who fails to give proper notice of taking or returning from maternity leave will be treated as being on unauthorised absence and liable to disciplinary action, but she will not forfeit her maternity rights.

10.10.5 PAYMENT DURING ORDINARY MATERNITY LEAVE

The employee is entitled to all benefits except pay. She may therefore receive all contractual benefits such as:

- Private health care.
- Use of the company car (if applicable).
- Accrued holiday.
- Pension contributions.
- Other service-related benefits.

The employee is entitled to the benefit of the terms and conditions of employment which would have applied if she had not been absent (other than pay) and she is bound by any obligations arising under those terms and conditions.

10.11 ADDITIONAL MATERNITY LEAVE PERIOD

A woman will only acquire the right to additional maternity leave in certain circumstances. To qualify she must:

- Have at least 1 year's continuous service by the start of the 11th week before the expected week of confinement; and
- Still be employed at that 11th qualifying week (she would still qualify if off sick with a pregnancy-related illness because the contract of employment would be live).

10.11.1 NOTIFICATION

The employee should provide advance notification to the employee in writing at least 21 days before the start of her maternity leave (unless not reasonably practicable in the circumstances) of the following:

- That she is pregnant.
- The expected week of confinement (normally confirmed with a medical certificate).
- The date when she wishes leave to commence.

If the employee gives birth before the date she has notified or before she has notified the employer at all, her maternity leave period will start automatically on the date of the birth.

If the employee is absent from work due to a pregnancy-related illness before the date she has notified the employer, her maternity leave period will begin automatically on the first day of absence following the beginning of the 6th week before the expected week of childbirth. Thereafter, she must notify her employer as soon as possible. Should the employee be away from work sick but the illness is unrelated to pregnancy, sick pay provisions will apply. If none exist other than the statutory sick pay scheme she may receive this benefit until her maternity leave commences. The period of leave will begin on the date she notifies the employer or if she has still to notify a date and gives birth, on the date of the birth.

10.11.2 THE ADDITIONAL MATERNITY LEAVE ENTITLEMENT

Provided she qualifies and complies with the requirements for notice, the employee will be entitled to additional maternity leave continuing until the end of 29 weeks beginning with the week in which the actual date of childbirth falls.

10.11.3 CHILDBIRTH

It is possible that a woman may give birth to a dead child. To take this factor into account the statutory provisions state that the definition of childbirth is the birth of a living child or the birth of a child whether living or dead after 24 weeks of pregnancy. Should a miscarriage occur before the end of the 24th week of pregnancy and the employee is off sick as a result she will not be regarded as absent through childbirth (although a dismissal for this absence may amount to sex discrimination – see Chapter 8). Ordinary contractual or statutory sick pay provisions will apply.

10.11.4 THE EMPLOYER REQUESTS CONFIRMATION OF RETURN

The employer is entitled to write to the employee on additional maternity leave to request written confirmation of the date on which childbirth occurred and that she still desires to return to work at the end of her additional maternity leave. This request cannot be made any earlier than 21 days before the end of her ordinary maternity leave period. If the employee still wishes to return she should respond to the request in writing within 21 days of receipt. This time limit cannot be extended and failure to respond means that the employee may fairly be disciplined. A warning of the consequences of failure to respond to the employer's request within 21 days of receiving it must be clearly stated in the employer's original letter of request.

10.11.5 EARLY RETURN

The employee can provide the employer with at least 21 days notice of her intended return date if she intends to return earlier than the end of her additional maternity leave period.

10.11.6 RETURN ON THE DUE DATE

Subject to section 10.11.4, an employee can simply present herself for work at the end of her additional maternity leave period.

10.11.7 CONTRACTUAL RIGHTS DURING ADDITIONAL MATERNITY LEAVE

The contract of employment continues during the additional leave period. The employee is entitled to the benefit of her employer's implied obligation to her of trust and confidence and any terms and conditions of her employment relating to:

- Notice of termination.
- Redundancy compensation.
- Disciplinary and grievance procedures.

Likewise, the employee is bound by her obligation to her employer of good faith and any terms and conditions of her employment relating to:

- Notice of termination.
- Disclosure of confidential information.
- Acceptance of gifts.
- Participation in any other business.

10.11.8 RESUMPTION OF WORK

The employee is entitled to return to the same job with the same terms and conditions of employment as if she had never been away from work. Furthermore, if in her absence there have been made any general improvements to the terms and conditions of employment by her employer, she is entitled to benefit as if she had been at work.

If a genuine redundancy situation has arisen whilst the employee was on maternity leave and her original job no longer exists, the employer or any associated employer must offer her a suitable alternative vacancy where one is available. The new job must be:

- Suitable and appropriate in the circumstances.
- On no less favourable terms than the original contract.

It will be regarded as an unfair dismissal if a suitable vacancy exists but the employer fails to offer it to the returning mother. If, for a reason other than redundancy, it is impracticable for the employee to return to her original position, she must be offered a suitable alternative vacancy and the same 2 conditions will apply. In practice, there is a very strong obligation on the employer to allow return to the same job – any comparable position will not do without an extremely good business reason.

As detailed in section 10.10.4, a woman who fails to return from additional maternity leave will be treated as being on unauthorised absence and liable to disciplinary action, but she will not forfeit her maternity rights.

10.11.9 SMALL EMPLOYERS

Businesses that employ less than 5 people (including employees of any associated employer) immediately before the end of the additional leave period are not subject to the automatic unfair dismissal provisions. This is provided that it is not reasonably practicable to permit the employee to return to a suitable job that is appropriate for her to do in the circumstances. To deny return legitimately they must be able to show why their action is reasonable and practicable in the circumstances. The employer must prove that return was not reasonably practicable if challenged.

10.12 RETURNING TO PART-TIME WORK

If the employer allows a request to return part-time, there is no problem in law and no break in service. The terms and conditions, in particular the hours, are deemed to have been varied by mutual agreement. However, the right to return is to the same job and that means in theory to the same hours as under the original contract. That said, the employer is under a duty to carefully consider the employee's request for less hours. If the request is rejected for no good reason the woman may bring a claim of indirect sex discrimination before an employment tribunal. She may bring this claim even where she returns to full-time work under sufferance.

Increasingly, employers are seen as acting in a discriminatory fashion for not considering or accommodating an employee's request in this regard. There must exist sound business reasons for refusal to allow part-time work to be justifiable.

10.13 BREAK IN EMPLOYMENT

The period of maternity leave will not break continuity of service and will count as service for the purpose of calculating statutory notice or redundancy entitlement.

10.14 MATERNITY SUSPENSION

An employee may be suspended from work on maternity grounds if a specified health and safety regulation prevents her from doing her normal tasks and duties because either:

* She is pregnant.
* She has recently given birth.
* She is breast feeding.

Should this occur the woman will have certain rights, which broadly are:

* To be offered any other suitable work available before being suspended.
* To be paid at her normal rate of pay for the duration of suspension – however long.
* Protection from dismissal because of a health and safety provision which does or could give rise to necessary maternity suspension.

These rights apply irrespective of the length of the employee's service or weekly hours. Any complaints in respect of the above may be made to an employment tribunal.

10.15 MATERNITY PAY

There are two entitlements to money for maternity. The first, Maternity Allowance (MA) is paid directly by the Department of Social Security. The second, Statutory Maternity Pay (SMP), is administered and paid by the employer (although, if not the whole, some of it can be recouped by the employer from National Insurance Contributions which would otherwise fall to be remitted). Broadly the difference between the two is the status of the woman, whether she is employed or unemployed.

10.15.1 MATERNITY ALLOWANCE

This is normally payable where:

- The woman is unemployed from the 11th week before the expected week of childbirth.
- The woman is employed or self-employed from a week of her choosing, but no earlier than the 11th week before the expected week of childbirth.

The entitlement to MA has conditions. These are:

- The woman must be pregnant and have reached, or been confined before reaching, the 11th week before the expected week of confinement.
- She must have been an employed or self-employed earner for at least 26 weeks in the 66 weeks ending with the week before the expected week of confinement.
- She must not be entitled to SMP.

The payment period is 18 weeks, payable any time after the 11th week before the expected week of confinement. The right to claim MA may be lost if the mother does not make the claim within 12 months of the birth. The rate of pay over that period is as follows:

- Standard rate – £60.20 per week.
- Lower rate – £52.25 per week.

The figures quoted in this section are subject to Government review in April each year.

10.15.2 STATUTORY MATERNITY PAY

Eligibility for SMP is dependent upon the employee fulfilling the following conditions:

- She must have been continuously employed by her employer for at least 26 weeks continuing into the 15th week before the expected week of confinement (the 15th week is known as the Qualifying Week (QW)).

- She must have stopped working for the employer wholly or partly as a result of pregnancy or confinement.
- She must have average weekly earnings of not less than the lower earnings limit in force at the time for payment of National Insurance Contributions for the period of 8 weeks ending with the QW (the current lower earnings limit is £67 per week).
- She must have become pregnant and still be pregnant at the beginning of the 11th week before the expected week of confinement, or have given birth.
- She must give 21 days notice to the employer that she intends to stop working because of her pregnancy.
- She must provide her employer with medical evidence for her expected week of confinement.

SMP is not conditional on an intention to return to work after the maternity leave.

10.15.3 THE QUALIFYING WEEK
This is simply calculated as the 15th week before the expected week of confinement.

10.15.4 CONTINUOUS SERVICE
Employment for any part of each of the 26 weeks will be sufficient to preserve continuity. The following will also count as continuous weeks of service:

- Where the employee is incapable of work due to sickness or injury.
- She is absent from work due to a temporary cessation of work.
- She is absent from work in circumstances that through the custom and practice of the employer are regarded as continuing employment.
- She is absent from work wholly or partly because of pregnancy or childbirth.

A transfer of a business resulting in a change in the woman's employer will also not affect continuity of service for the purposes of SMP.

10.15.5 MEDICAL EVIDENCE
SMP can only be paid where the employer is in receipt of evidence of the expected date of confinement. This is usually complied with by providing for the employer form MAT B1 (Certificate of Maternity).

10.15.6 PAYMENT
SMP is regarded as earnings and will therefore attract tax and National Insurance contribution deductions. It may be paid on the employee's normal pay days for the duration of the payment period or paid in a lump sum.

10.15.7 THE MATERNITY PAY PERIOD

SMP is payable for an 18 week period. It only becomes a shorter period if:

- The woman is taken into legal custody.
- She goes outside countries which are members of the European Union or the European Free Trade Agreement.
- She dies.
- She works during the period.

In general, when it starts depends upon when the employee gives notice and stops work (see section 10.15.8)

10.15.8 WORKING DURING THE PERIOD

The woman does not have to leave employment at the 15th week before the expected week of confinement. She could carry on working right up to childbirth provided no health and safety regulations restrain her. The first week of the period may not be earlier than the 11th week before the expected week of confinement, nor later than the first week that immediately follows confinement. It may be in the woman's interest financially to continue working for as long as possible given the rate of SMP she is to receive as compared to her wage or salary.

10.15.9 THE RATES OF SMP

There are 2, the lower and higher rate.

1. The lower rate – £60.20 per week.
2. The higher rate – 90 per cent of the average weekly wage.

The higher rate is payable for a maximum of 6 weeks, the lower rate then becomes payable for up to the remaining 12 weeks of the period. The lower rate is subject to Government review in April each year.

10.16 MISCELLANEOUS POINTS ON SMP

10.16.1 NON-PAYMENT

If the employer decides not to pay or to stop paying SMP, the woman is entitled to reasons for the decision provided for her on form SMP1. Disputes over non-payment go before an Inland Revenue Officer for a formal decision. Appeal against their decision lies to a Tax Commissioner.

10.16.2 MULTIPLE BIRTHS

One amount of SMP only is payable irrespective of how many babies are expected by the mother.

10.16.3 MULTIPLE EMPLOYERS

Provided the employee qualifies according to the payment rules, there is nothing in theory to prevent SMP being payable by two or more employers.

10.16.4 INSOLVENCY

Where SMP is payable but the employer becomes insolvent, the liability for payment will rest with the Secretary of State. In other words, the employee's entitlement is assured.

10.17 CONTRACTUAL MATERNITY ENTITLEMENTS

This chapter has concentrated on the statutory rights in respect of maternity. That is, what represents the 'floor of rights' beneath which the employer may not go. However, there are a number of employers who are willing to provide entitlements to both leave and pay over and above the statutory minimum. As with all contractual matters this may occur through express provision of the contract of employment, oral agreement or be implied through custom and practice as a term and condition of employment. In such cases, the statutory provision becomes a 'fall-back' position for the employee that may or may not need to be relied upon. Should enhanced contractual entitlements exist, but be breached by the employer, the employee's remedy is one for damages for breach of contract before an employment tribunal, county court or High Court, depending on the amount in dispute.

10.18 PARENTAL LEAVE

From 15 December 1999, there is a new right of parental leave, introduced in order to comply with the EU Parental Leave Directive. The law entitles an employee to be absent from work on parental leave in order to care for a natural or an adopted child. The main provisions of the parental leave scheme are:

- A right for natural mothers and fathers (as named on the child's birth certificate) and adoptive mothers and fathers to each take up to 13 weeks unpaid time off work to care for a child during the first five years of its life (or the first five years after adoption, up to age 18). The right applies to children born after 15 December 1999 or children under 18 adopted after that date. Parents who have acquired formal parental responsibility for a child born after 15 December who is under five years old also qualify. In the case of twins, 13 weeks' leave must be provided for each child.
- Parents of disabled children born after 15 December 1999 are able to use their entitlement to 13 weeks' unpaid leave over a longer period, up until the child's 18th birthday. A disabled child is a child for whom disability living allowance is awarded.
- Employees qualify if they have one years' continuous service with their employer.
- The employee remains employed while on parental leave, his job must be kept open and he must not lose any of his seniority and pension rights that he had built up before taking parental leave.

- The employer is not required to keep records, but he can reasonably ask for evidence to support a request for parental leave.
- When an employee changes jobs, employers are free to make enquiries of a previous employer or seek a declaration from the employee about how much parental leave he has taken. If an employee behaves dishonestly in claiming entitlement to parental leave, the employer is entitled to take disciplinary action.

The Government has proposed a "fallback scheme" for parental leave, which will automatically apply in the absence of employers and employees agreeing their own scheme in a collective or workforce agreement and then giving the scheme legal force by writing it into employee's contracts of employment. The key elements above must be part of any agreed scheme, although it can be more generous. For example, employees must be able to take the equivalent of 13 weeks' leave, whether the agreed scheme allows this to be in days, weeks, one long block or as reduced working hours or a mixture of all of these. Subject to this requirement, collective or workforce agreements can set aside the Model Scheme and replace it with a different set of arrangements entirely. Arrangements can cover matters such as how much notice of parental leave must be given, arrangements for postponing leave when the business cannot cope, and how it should be taken.

If no scheme is agreed, the fallback scheme also provides the following:

- Leave must be taken in blocks of one week, up to a maximum of four weeks' leave in a year (for each child). If leave is to care for a disabled child, leave may be taken a day at a time or longer if they wish.
- 21 days' notice must be given by the employee.
- The employer can postpone leave where the operation of the employer's business would be unduly disrupted by the employee taking leave, but not for more than six months. The employer should confirm the postponement arrangements in writing no later than 7 days after the employer's notice to take leave and the employer's notice should state the reason for postponement and set out the new dates of parental leave.
- Leave cannot be postponed when an employee gives notice to take it immediately after the time the child is born or placed with the family for adoption.

An employee may complain to an employment tribunal where his employer has unreasonably postponed a period of parental leave or has prevented him from taking parental leave. Employees also have the right not to be subjected to any detriment for reasons relating to parental leave and any dismissal on these grounds is automatically unfair and not subject to a service requirement.

10.19 TIME OFF FOR FAMILY EMERGENCIES

In addition to parental leave, from 15 December 1999, there is a new right to take a reasonable amount of time off work to deal with family emergencies. This is **unpaid** leave. The Government has given the following examples of cases which will be covered:

- To provide assistance or make arrangements for the provision of care if a dependant falls ill, is injured or assaulted, or gives birth.
- Dealing with the consequences of the death of a dependent e.g. dealing with funeral arrangements and attending the funeral.
- Dealing with the consequences of a child being involved in an incident at school or during school hours.
- Where child care, or other arrangements for the care of a dependant, break down.

For these purposes, a 'dependant' generally means a spouse, child, parent or a person living in the employee's household as part of the family. In the first and last example of cases covered, "dependant" also includes any person who reasonably relies on the employee for assistance, or to make arrangements for the provision of care, in the event of illness or injury.

The employee is obliged to tell his employer the reason for his absence as soon as reasonably practicable and how long he expects to be absent. An employee may complain to an employment tribunal where his employer has failed to permit him to take time off. Employees also have the right not to be subjected to any detriment for reasons relating to time off for family emergencies and any dismissal on these grounds is automatically unfair and not subject to a service requirement.

10.20 CASE STUDY

Joanna is employed by Richard, the owner of 'Lovely Motor Used Car Emporium' and has 8 months' service. She is 6 months pregnant. She is unsure of her entitlement to leave and maternity pay and whenever she asks Richard his smooth-talking fails to provide her with either answers or reassurance. Joanna would also like to return to work on reduced hours once the baby is born. She seeks legal advice.

Joanna will not have 1 years' service as at the 11th week before the expected week of confinement (EWC) and will, therefore, only be entitled to ordinary maternity leave of 18 weeks. This leave may commence any time after the 11th week before the EWC. When Joanna chooses to commence leave she will be entitled to statutory maternity pay (SMP) for the duration of the leave; the first 6 weeks at 90% of her pay and the remaining 12 weeks at the lower rate of SMP — currently £60.20.

She should notify Richard of the date she wishes to commence leave at least 21 days beforehand. Joanna's contract of employment will continue throughout her maternity leave and she will be entitled to all contractual benefits during leave, for example, her company car, private health care payment and employer's pension contribution. She will also continue to accrue holiday entitlement whilst on leave.

With regard to her wish to return to work part-time, she is advised to raise this with Richard at the earliest opportunity. Richard must carefully consider her request and must not reject it out of hand. Richard must accommodate a part-time return where there is no good business reason to refuse her request. If the job requires full-time hours, Richard should also consider the possibility of a job share.

CHAPTER ELEVEN
TRANSFER OF UNDERTAKINGS

11.1 INTRODUCTION

Until the 1970s, where a business changed hands and passed from one owner to another, the employees of the business being purchased had no employment protection. They would be terminated and made redundant or, if fortunate, the new owner may offer them similar jobs. What was never certain was whether any work would be offered at all and if it was, the terms and conditions could be quite different and continuity of service broken. The situation, as recognised by European Community, was less than ideal. As a result, the United Kingdom enacted the Transfer of Undertakings (Protection of Employment) Regulations 1981 (TUPE) in order to give effect to the European Acquired Rights Directive.

These provisions apply in cases where a business (undertaking) is transferred from one owner to another, usually by sale, and whether the owner is an individual, partner or limited company. They do not apply where the transfer is effected between the parties by the passing of shares only. In short, TUPE provides protection for all employees who are to be transferred as part of a going concern that is to be passed to a new owner.

11.2 THE EMPLOYEE'S RIGHTS UPON TRANSFER

- Where an undertaking is transferred from employer A to employer B, the employee's of A automatically become the employee's of B from the time of the transfer.
- Transferred employees are deemed employees of employer B on the same terms and conditions of employment as they enjoyed with employer A.
- Employer B becomes responsible for any rights and liabilities in respect of the transferred employees.
- Collective agreements made between employer A and a recognised trade union will transfer to employer B. Employer B must comply with their requirements.
- Where employer A recognised a trade union and, following the transfer, the part of the business transferred is distinctly different from any other owned by employer B, B must recognise the union in respect of those employees.
- Employer A must inform any recognised trade unions about the consequences of the transfer and employer B must provide A with sufficient information in this respect.
- In certain defined circumstances (see later), it may be necessary for both or either employer A and B to consult with recognised trade unions or employee representatives in respect of the transfer.

- Should an employee be dismissed for any reason connected with the transfer it will be deemed to be an automatically unfair dismissal unless it is an economic, technical or organisational reason entailing changes in the workplace. If it is for one of those reasons, the dismissal may be fair and reasonable depending on the facts and circumstances of the case.

11.3 'EMPLOYEES' UNDER THE REGULATIONS

The definition of 'employee' for the purposes of the Regulations is wider than in the context of many other pieces of protective legislation. It includes:

- Full-time workers.
- Part-time workers.
- Workers under a fixed-term contract which has not yet expired.
- Servants.
- Apprentices.

It may include:

- Casual workers.
- Seasonal workers.
- Agency-supplied workers.

Whether or not these categories are protected by the Regulations has yet to be firmly established by case law. It does not include independent contractors (under a contract for the supply of services).

11.4 'UNDERTAKINGS' UNDER THE REGULATIONS

Until an amendment in 1993, the Regulations did not apply to any undertaking (business) which was not in the nature of a commercial venture. This meant, for example, that employees transferred between charitable businesses were not protected by the provision of the Regulations. Since 1993 this position has changed and 'undertaking' is now defined as including any 'trade or business'.

An undertaking may also be part of a trade or business, provided the part being purchased by employer B is distinct, severable and self-contained from the remainder of the vendor's business. For example:

Company A manufactures and produces furniture. This furniture is delivered to retailers using company A's fleet of delivery vans which employs van drivers solely for this task. Company B is a specialist delivery service and it buys company A's delivery division including the vehicles, drivers and book of business. In this situation the delivery function of company A is likely to be regarded as an undertaking that is a distinct and severable part of the furniture production business. It follows that the van drivers transferred to company B could expect to be protected by the Regulations.

In addition to charities now being regarded as undertakings, so too are professional practices such as solicitors, doctors and accountants. The test is now whether the trade or business is an 'economic entity' in its own right.

11.5 WHAT IS A TRANSFER?

The answer to this question requires the assessment of two matters;

1. The various means by which the transfer of ownership can be effected.
2. Whether an 'economic entity' has been acquired which retains its identity after the transfer, or merely certain physical assets which belonged to the undertaking or part of it.

11.6 TRANSFER MECHANISMS

Dealing with the first issue, the Regulations state that they will apply whether the transfer is effected by the sale or by some other disposition or by operation of law. There are 3 mechanisms for transferring ownership which between them cover almost all forms by which business ownership can be transferred.

11.6.1 SALE

This is the most common and simplistic form of transfer and requires no further explanation.

11.6.2 'SOME OTHER DISPOSITION'

This will include a valid gift of an operational business to another. Another common example is where a business activity relates intrinsically to land under a business lease. Should the lease be granted, terminated, surrendered or assigned this will lead to a disposition. If a business changes hands in this way and continues to be run as essentially the same business, then the Regulations will apply. Other transfers caught under this section include those in relation to franchises, licenses and concessions.

11.6.3 'OPERATION OF LAW'

The transfer of a business by 'operation of law' involves some sort of automatic legal process applying to effect the legal transfer from one employer to another. Typically, this could include automatic succession from a deceased sole trader to a personal representative on the expiry of a commercial lease and its automatic reversion to the landlord. For the Regulations to apply in similar situations it is necessary, further to the automatic transfer,   that the business will carry on as a going concern by the person who now finds themselves the employer and owner as a result of the change.

11.7 TERRITORIAL LIMITS

The Regulations apply to a transfer from employer A to employer B of an undertaking situated in the UK. They apply even where the transfer is governed or effected by foreign law or if the employees of the business work outside the UK or their employment is governed by foreign law. However, the theoretical geographical extent of the Regulations is limited in practice by the application of the unfair dismissal provisions that do not normally apply where the employee ordinarily works outside the UK.

11.8 'ECONOMIC ENTITY'

For the Regulations to apply, it is critical that any transferred undertaking retains its distinct identity as it continues with the recipient of the business (employer B). All the facts and circumstances must be considered. In particular, the following factors will be important:

- The type of business.
- Whether any tangible assets such as buildings, machinery and vehicles have been transferred.
- Whether any goodwill was assigned or acquired.
- The transfer of employees.
- The transfer of customers.
- The transfer of business orders.
- The similarity of activity carried on by employer B after the transfer.
- Any period in which business activity was suspended.
- Whether a 'going concern' has been transferred.

11.8.1 GOODWILL

Many cases in this area of law have indicated that goodwill is an important factor in deciding whether a business has been transferred. However, it is inherently difficult to define. It obviously includes the reputation of the business and its value in respect of staff, customers and suppliers. It is an intangible asset of the business. Indications of goodwill having been transferred where there exists no express assignment are:

- The transfer of work in progress.
- The promise of employer A to employer B to assist the latter in the retention of customers.
- A restriction placed on employer A by employer B to prevent A from setting up in competition.
- The transfer of customers and clients.
- The retention by employer B of the business name.
- The transfer of brand names and/or trademarks.
- The transfer of employees themselves.

It follows that where it can be reasonably assessed that the goodwill of the business has been transferred, employees may use this as a fairly reliable indication of a transfer as defined by the Regulations. As such, their employment service and terms and conditions should be afforded statutory protection. It must be added that no two situations are identical and no one factor on its own assures a definitive transfer situation. The facts and circumstances of each particular case must be assessed on their own merit.

11.9 CONTRACTING-OUT

The most recent addition to the list of situations where there is deemed to be an effective transfer of an undertaking concerns the contracting-out of services that until that point in time have been done 'in-house' and changes of contractors. The most common examples are in respect of cleaning and catering services. For example:

Where employer A retains cleaning staff in-house and then decides for a business reason to contract out the cleaning to employer B, a cleaning services specialist provider, there will be a transfer of an undertaking in law in most cases. That means that the employees of employer A who were engaged to perform cleaning duties must be taken on by employer B with their continuity of service, terms and conditions of employment remaining unaffected. Employees who are being told they are redundant from employer A in similar circumstances should be aware of their right to claim the protection of the Regulations. It may well be that there is no redundancy, merely a change of employer.

The transfer of an undertaking must involve the transfer of a stable economic entity that retains its identity, meaning an organised grouping of resources which has the objective of pursuing an economic activity.

11.10 SHARE TRANSFERS

As the law currently stands, employees are afforded no statutory protection by the Regulations in respect of the transfer of shares in a company which carries on the undertaking. The reasoning is that the legal identity of a corporate employer does not change merely because of a change in the identity of the principal shareholders. The change in shareholding has no impact on the contractual relationship between the employees and their employing company. What changes by share transfer is the control of the company which moves into different hands.

11.11 THE TIME OF THE TRANSFER

The timing of the transfer and dismissals effected by the employer were used, in the past, as a mechanism for avoiding liability for unfair dismissal. The situation is now quite clear – timing the transfer and dismissals will not prevent a relevant employee from having a potential claim for unfair dismissal where the reason for termination is connected with the transfer. A broad approach to the right to make a claim has therefore been adopted by the courts.

11.12 INSOLVENCY AND HIVING DOWN

Companies which are forced into receivership or liquidation very often have profitable parts of their business. 'Hiving down' provisions exist in law to attract buyers to the viable parts of the business, which is seen to be in the best interests of the creditors. Where a receiver, liquidator or administrator of a company transfers the business of the company to a wholly-owned subsidiary for the purposes of hiving down, the Regulations do not apply unless either:

- The subsidiary ceases to be wholly owned; or
- The business is transferred from the subsidiary to a third party.

These provisions prevent the automatic transfer of staff to the hived down company. In turn, this allows a potential purchaser to buy a part of the original business free from the encumbrances and liabilities that apply to the existing staff. The business is effectively separated from the employees engaged in it.

Often the receiver appointed will continue to run the entire company as a going concern with a view to selling the whole business. Currently the receiver has a 'window' of 14 days from appointment in which to hive down or otherwise dispose of the original employees free from potential liability for unfair dismissal. Once the 14 days has elapsed, the receiver is deemed to be the new employer and any disposal of staff thereafter must be fair and reasonable. Should an employee be unfairly dismissed after the 14 day period they may bring a claim in respect of the same, directly against the receiver.

11.13 THE CONTRACT OF EMPLOYMENT – AUTOMATIC ASSIGNMENT

The Regulations are drafted with the intention of preventing a break in continuity of employment and to pass liability at the point of transfer on to the purchaser of the business. They state that the vendor's employees will automatically become, from the point in time of the transfer, employees of the purchaser on the same terms and conditions of employment as those enjoyed with the vendor. This only applies to those who were employed immediately before the transfer of the business, and whose contracts would otherwise have been terminated by the transfer (a reference to the old law - see section 11.1). The reference to 'immediately before the transfer' is not to be taken literally and no technical termination before the transfer will deny a dismissed employee the right to claim the protection of the Regulations.

11.14 THE EMPLOYEE OBJECTS TO THE TRANSFER

Special provisions exist to allow an employee not to be transferred to another employer against their will. If the employee objects to the transfer this will act to terminate their contract of employment with the vendor at the point of transfer. This is not viewed as a dismissal, consequently no notice or redundancy pay is payable and the employee may not claim unfair dismissal.

11.15 'NEW' EMPLOYMENT WITH THE PURCHASER

As detailed in this chapter, the employee's terms and conditions of employment roll-over intact from employer A to employer B as a result of the transfer. Their rights are protected. In practice, the purchaser is often left with a new workforce that has different terms and conditions of employment from their own existing staff. Employees should expect, over a period of time, the new employer to seek to harmonise terms and conditions of employment across the whole workforce. That said, each contract of employment is individual and the contract should not be altered in any way by the new employer without the express agreement of the employee further to consultation. Failure to seek agreement and to impose changes unilaterally could lead to a breach of contract by the new employer. The employee would have the right to claim damages for breach of contract or, if the change was fundamental in nature and the employee had 1 years' service, a claim for constructive dismissal could be considered.

The opposite side of the equation is where the new employer's existing staff has terms and conditions which are far more favourable. In this situation the transferred employee has no right to demand the benefit of these terms and conditions. The new employer inherits all rights and liabilities. This means that if employer A owed money to the staff under contract, the new employer B would be liable to those staff to discharge the debt. However, criminal liabilities are not assigned to employer B under the Regulations.

Finally, continuity of employment is preserved under the Regulations. This allows the transferred employee to regard all their previous continuous service with employer A as continuous service with employer B. The contract of employment continues unbroken and any accrued rights such as the right to a statutory redundancy payment or to claim unfair dismissal (after 1 years' service) will be unaffected by the fact of the transfer of the business.

11.16 PENSIONS

Terms and conditions relating to the provision of occupational pensions in respect of old age, invalidity or survivors are excluded from the Regulations. The purchaser of a business takes it free from any such pension provisions and will not be acting unlawfully if they fail or refuse to maintain the same terms and conditions in relation to such schemes.

11.17 TRANSFER AND TRADE UNIONS

Where they exist, collective agreements are deemed to be automatically transferred to the business purchaser. The position or transfer may be clear enough, but it should be remembered that most collective agreements are not legally enforceable contracts, they are matters of custom, practice and recognition. However, if the terms of the collective agreement are incorporated into a transferring employee's contract of employment, then its term will bind the purchaser because he has inherited the rights and liabilities in the employee's contract.

11.17.1 CONSULTATION

Under the Regulations, any employer in a union-recognition environment must inform union representatives, in enough time before the transfer to enable consultation in respect of the following:

- The fact of an imminent transfer.
- The expected date of transfer.
- The reasons for the transfer.
- The legal, economic and social implications of the transfer upon the relevant employees.
- The measures the employer intends to take further to the transfer in respect of the employees.
- The measures which the purchaser intends to take further to the transfer in respect of the employees.

If either the vendor or the purchaser envisages taking measures in relation to any of the affected employees, consultation must be with a view to seeking the union's agreement to the measures to be taken. There exists, therefore, a clear obligation to meaningfully consult with union representatives at the earliest practical moment once the decision to transfer is apparent. Should the employer fail to do this, the union may present a complaint to an employment tribunal within 3 months after the date of transfer. This limitation may be extended if it can be shown why an earlier complaint was not reasonably practicable. The tribunal is empowered to make a declaration that the obligation to consult has been breached and to order the employer to pay compensation to the employees involved. The maximum amount payable is 13 weeks' pay for each employee affected. The employer may seek to defend their liability in this regard by pleading 'special circumstances'. In practice, this defence is rarely accepted by a tribunal.

Where there is no recognised union, consultation is required with employee representatives and an employer may choose between:

- Already elected employee representatives, (provided that they are deemed to have the authority of the affected employees bearing in mind the 'purposes for and method by which they were appointed or elected'); or
- Employee representatives specifically elected for the purpose of a TUPE transfer, provided that the process of their election complies with the requirements set out in the legislation.

The legislation sets out criteria that must be satisfied in relation to an election of employee representatives. These include ensuring that all affected employees are entitled to vote and that none of the affected employees are unreasonably excluded from standing for election. The voting process should be secret.

The employer is able to determine the number of representatives to be elected, and their term of office (subject to enabling the information/consultation process to be properly completed). The employer can also decide whether the employees should be represented by a representative for a particular class of employees, or by a representative/s for the entire group.

Complaints can also be made by either the representatives or the affected employees to a tribunal. The onus is on the employer to show, where appropriate, that the employee representatives had the authority to represent the employees and/or that the election requirements were satisfied.

Employees who participate in an election of employee representatives are not to be dismissed, or subjected to a detriment, on that ground alone.

Employee representatives, and trade union officials, are entitled to time off during working hours for training to perform their functions in relation to consultation.

11.18 DISMISSAL

Provided there is a connection between the reason for dismissal and the event of the transfer, such dismissals will be regarded by the Regulations as automatically unfair, regardless of how reasonably or unreasonably the employer behaved. It is immaterial whether or not the dismissals are before or after the transfer. Unfair dismissal may be claimed in the following transfer circumstances:

- Where the employee is transferred from the employment of employer A to employer B but employer B substantially changes the existing terms and conditions of employment to the employee's detriment and the employee resigns as a result.
- The employee is dismissed prior to the transfer by employer A.
- The employee is dismissed prior to the transfer by employer A at the request of employer B.
- The employee is retained after the transfer but subsequently dismissed by employer B for a reason connected to the transfer.
- The employee is dismissed by employer B immediately after the transfer, for a reason connected with the transfer.
- An employee in employer B's own workforce is dismissed before or after the transfer as a result of a redundancy or reorganisation caused by accommodating the new employees of employer A.

Whether or not the dismissal is connected with the transfer is a matter of fact for the tribunal in many cases. Usually dismissals which take place close to the time of the transfer are presumed to be connected with it but this is no more than a rule of thumb. It is also not beyond possibility that a dismissal many weeks or even months after the date of transfer could still be regarded as connected with the transfer and therefore automatically unfair.

It does seem that the courts expect new employers to properly and rationally restructure and reorganise their workforce at some time after transfer. If this is done logically for sound business reasons, the situation having been monitored for some time post-transfer, it is very likely that subsequent dismissals will be potentially fair and the connection with the transfer successfully broken. What the courts will not accept is the treatment of employees as a mere commodity to be crudely handled by employers as part of a business transaction (see Chapter 4).

11.19 THE 'ECONOMIC, TECHNICAL OR ORGANISATIONAL REASON' DEFENCE (ETO)

This defence may seem a 'great escape' for the employers but in practice it is very narrowly construed by the courts. The key to the defence is the second limb which states that the ETO reason must 'entail changes in the workforce'. Proving an ETO reason is not sufficient in itself, the employer must show some sort of imperative behind the dismissal. The change to the workforce must be an objective of the transfer business plan and not merely a consequence of it. The reorganisation must be planned with the resultant dismissals being a deliberate and necessary feature of the employer's plan.

The obligation to plan business restructuring is placed firmly on the employer before the ETO defence may be sustained, but in practice greatly limits the working and effect of the defence. Most employers negotiating transfers are working within time scales and other commercial considerations that just do not afford the required level of planning to be undertaken. This is to the advantage of the employee and why in most transfer situations the ETO defence fails and employment rights are protected by the Regulations. Even where an ETO defence is sustained, the employer must also act reasonably in all the circumstances in treating the reason as sufficiently justifying dismissal. The ETO reason to be examined is that of the employer who dismisses the employee.

11.20 TRANSFER AND DISMISSAL FOR REDUNDANCY

Where there is an effective transfer of an undertaking there is no termination of the contract of employment and therefore no dismissal in law. If there is no dismissal there can be no redundancy since redundancy is a reason for dismissal. However, those dismissals that take place before or after the transfer, but are not held to be unfair because of their lack of connection with the transfer, are likely to be genuine redundancy situations. This is brought about by the necessary changes and restructuring of the business at some time before or after the transfer. The employee will qualify for statutory redundancy payments where the reason for dismissal falls into the ETO reasons defence as detailed in section 11.19.

11.21 AGREEMENT TO AVOID THE REGULATIONS

Any attempt to seek to avoid the application and consequences of the Regulations by private arrangement between the employer and employee or between vendor and purchaser, will be unlawful and the agreement invalid.

11.22 CASE STUDY

John is a sales manager for Edward's TV Production Company 'Kings Road Creations'. John has 6 years' service and is a member of a twenty-strong team employed by Edward. 'Big Shot Productions', a competitor of Edward's, have made him an offer for his business. It is an offer Edward cannot refuse and he is keen to negotiate an agreement for sale. Helen, an ex glamour model turned entrepreneur, owns Big Shot Productions and is known in the business as a ruthless operator.

Helen insists that there will be no deal with Edward unless John is made redundant before the transfer of his business to her. Helen says the reason is that she already has a sales manager who is far more effective than John. Edward, in fear of losing the deal, approaches John and makes him redundant 2 days prior to the transfer of his business to Helen. John is paid his statutory redundancy entitlements. Understandably, John is distraught and seeks legal advice.

The transfer of Edward's business to Helen was the sale of a going concern and was, quite clearly, an economic entity. It is, therefore, a relevant transfer for the purposes of the Regulations. John has been dismissed 'further to' the transfer that is, had it not been for the transfer, his employment with Edward would have continued. John's dismissal does not come within the potential ETO defence (see 11.19) because it was not part of a planned restructure prior to the transfer, it was a dismissal at the request of the transferee (Helen). There was no imperative 'entailing changes in the workforce', merely a wish by Edward to sell to Helen for the best price.

John's dismissal is automatically unfair and since he has more than 1 years' service he may bring his claim before the employment tribunal. John's legal action is against Helen, the recipient of Kings Road Creations, not Edward. It is not practical for John to claim reinstatement but his claim for compensation is successful and he is awarded £17,000. Although this award is made against Helen's business and she is liable to pay it, she proves worthy of her ruthless reputation. She had an indemnity clause drafted into the contract of sale of Edward's business entitling her to claim against him personally for any losses suffered as a result of John's action.

CHAPTER TWELVE
HEALTH AND SAFETY

12.1 THE COMMON LAW DUTY

There are many statutes which seek to protect an employee's health and safety whilst in employment and these will be dealt with later in this chapter. In addition, the common law places a duty on all employers to take such steps as are reasonable and necessary to ensure the safety of their employees. If the employer fails in their duty they will have committed a wrong against the employee who is injured or killed as a result of their employer's negligence. The claim will be for damages.

In order to further protect employees who may suffer at the hands of their employer, the law requires all employers (irrespective of the size of the business) to have Employer's Liability Insurance. As a result, should the employee have a claim against the employer it is in practice brought against their insurer who must meet or defend the claim.

The duty of care employers owe to their employees is measured by the application of the following test which requires the employer to provide:

* A safe place of work.
* A safe means of access to their place of work.
* A safe system of work.
* Adequate equipment and materials.
* Competent fellow employees.
* Protection to employees against unnecessary risk of injury.

Should the employer fail in any of the above, the employee who has suffered as a result is likely to have a reasonable claim for damages.

12.1.1 SAFE PLACE OF WORK

The employer's premises must be in good repair and regularly inspected. Premises which are normally safe can become temporarily unsafe. For example, if oil is spilt on the workshop floor and is not cleaned up promptly or properly. If the employer sends an employee to another place of work (for example, to a contractor's premises) they have a general duty to check that place of work to ensure it is safe for their employees, in so far as is reasonably practicable. This duty cannot be delegated to the contractor.

12.1.2 SAFE MEANS OF ACCESS

This means that approach paths, private roads and thoroughfares at the place of work or on the employer's premises must be safe for the employees coming to and from work. For example, failure to remove ice on a footpath within the work site which causes injury would be a breach of this duty.

12.1.3 SAFE SYSTEM OF WORK

This, in essence, requires the method used to undertake the work to be safe. Short-cut procedures, which increase productivity at the expense of health and safety considerations, will not be a safe system of work. The employer is afforded a defence provided they can show that they have taken all reasonable steps to ensure that a safe system of work is in operation.

12.1.4 SAFE EQUIPMENT AND MATERIALS

This includes the provision of safety equipment for employees where appropriate. Materials delivered to a workplace should be checked for safety and any defects that may cause harm to employees who would handle them in their normal course of work.

12.1.5 COMPETENT FELLOW WORKERS

Should an employer hire an incompetent, inexperienced or unqualified co-worker whose actions cause injury to another employee, the employer is likely to have breached this duty of care.

12.1.6 PROTECTION FROM INJURY

The employer is under a duty to do all that is reasonably possible in the circumstances to eliminate risks at the workplace.

12.2 VICARIOUS LIABILITY

The principle of vicarious liability acts to make an employer liable for the negligent acts of any of their employees committed whilst in the course of their duty. This would mean that a hammer dropped due to carelessness by one employee on to another's foot and causing injury, could lead to a claim by the injured party directly against the employer under this principle. Each case will depend on its own facts and circumstances. There is no vicarious liability if the negligent act committed by the employee is so far removed from what he is authorised to do, that he can be said to be on "a frolic of his own".

12.3 THE OCCUPIER'S LIABILITY ACT 1957

Under this Act, amongst others, the employer is under a legal duty to their employees to:

> *"Take such care as in all the circumstances of the case is reasonable to see that the (employee) is reasonably safe in using the premises for the purposes"... of their work.*

12.4 THE WORKPLACE (HEALTH AND SAFETY AND WELFARE) REGULATIONS 1992

The employer is under a duty to the employee (among others) in the interests of general health and welfare to ensure that their factory and other work premises are:

- Clean.
- Not overcrowded.
- At a minimum temperature.
- Well ventilated.
- Well drained.
- Well lit.
- Able to provide fresh drinking water.
- Able to provide washing facilities.
- Able to provide accommodation for clothing and seating.
- Able to provide adequately fenced machinery.
- Safe for access.
- Generally well maintained.
- Safe in respect of dangerous substances.

12.4.1 ENFORCEMENT

An employee may claim for any breach under the Regulations provided always that they can establish that the breach caused the accident and injury. The Health and Safety Executive (see later) is empowered to enforce the provisions of the Regulations.

12.5 CONTRIBUTORY NEGLIGENCE

As with all common law actions for negligence, the amount of damages an injured employee may be awarded by a court, must take into account whether they committed any contributory negligence. That is, in some way, failed to take reasonable steps to ensure their own safety. Where there is deemed to be some element of contributory negligence the court may reduce the award accordingly by a percentage – this can in theory be by anything up to 100%.

12.6 THE HEALTH AND SAFETY AT WORK ACT 1974

This Act has been effectively described as an attempt to balance the degree of risk to employees welfare against the cost and reasonable ability of the employer to minimise that risk. It follows that under the provisions of the Act a number of duties are placed on the employers.

12.7 EMPLOYER'S DUTIES

They are as follows:

- The employer is under a general duty to ensure, in so far as is reasonably practicable, the health, safety and welfare of all their employees.
- They must provide and maintain plant and systems of work that are safe.
- Arrangements must be made to ensure safety and minimise risk with regard to the use, handling, storage and transport of articles and substances.

- The employer must provide all employees with such information, instruction, training and supervision necessary to ensure health and safety at the workplace.
- The place of work must be well maintained and kept in a safe condition, including access to and from that place, in order that it presents no risk to the health and safety of the employees.
- The provision and maintenance of a working environment which is safe and without risk to health and has adequate facilities and arrangements for the staff.

Broadly, the Act is designed to give statutory force to the common law duty of care an employer owes their employees.

12.7.1 HEALTH AND SAFETY POLICY STATEMENT

Employers are under an obligation to provide a general written policy with regard to the health and safety at work of their employees and the arrangements for carrying out that policy. The content of the policy must include:

- A general statement of policy concerning health and safety.
- Organisational arrangements for implementing the policy.
- Identification of specific hazards and a statement of the rules designed to deal with them.

Such information must actively be brought to the notice of the employees. However, employers with fewer than five employees are exempted from the obligation to provide a policy statement.

12.7.2 SAFETY REPRESENTATIVES

Safety representatives and safety committees must be appointed and constituted respectively where a trade union is recognised and a collective agreement exists between employer and the employee's union. Employers must allow safety representatives time off with pay to perform the functions of investigating potential hazards and complaints about the health and safety or welfare of any employee or group of employees. Safety representatives should be regarded as points of health and safety information. They may make representations to the employer, represent the employees in consultation with inspectors of the Health and Safety Executive and conduct inspections of the workplace.

12.8 EMPLOYEE'S DUTIES

All employees whilst at work have a duty to:

- Take reasonable care for their own health and safety and of other persons who may be affected by their acts or omissions at work.
- Co-operate with their employer in ensuring that requirements or duties imposed on the employer in law are complied with.

For example, if an employee's job includes lifting heavy items and the employer has provided steel toe-capped boots for their general health and safety, the employee is under a duty to wear the protective footwear provided.

12.9 EMPLOYEE INTERFERENCE WITH SAFETY MEASURES

If an employee deliberately or recklessly interferes with health and safety measures provided by the employer, they may be guilty of a criminal offence which may be punished by a fine unlimited in law.

12.10 PROVISION OF SAFETY EQUIPMENT

Given the nature of the duty imposed on employers to take all reasonable precautions and to provide all reasonable apparatus to minimise the risk to the health and safety of their workforce, it follows that this can be costly financially. The law does not permit the cost of health and safety items to be passed on to the employee by the employer. Should the employer force the employee to pay for their own safety equipment, the employee should complain to the local Health and Safety Executive office (see later Useful Addresses).

12.11 ACCIDENTS AT WORK

Any employee who suffers an injury in the course of their work which results in them being incapable of work for four consecutive days or more must report the accident to the employer. The report may be orally or in writing. Normally reporting will lead to information being recorded in an 'accident book' which all employers with more than ten employees are required to keep at the workplace. In the following circumstances, to allow for proper independent investigation, the employer is under a duty to report to the Health and Safety Executive:

- Any accident which results in the employee being off work for more than three days.
- Any accident which results in the death or major injury of an employee.
- Any notifiable dangerous occurrence.
- The death of an employee within one year of being injured as the result of a notifiable accident or dangerous occurrence.
- Any suffering by an employee of a specified work-related disease.
- Incidents relating to gas release.

Any employee who is injured severely or suffers serious illness whilst at work or as a result of work should check with the local Health and Safety Executive Office to see whether they received any notification from their employer. The inspection carried out by the Executive could assist the employee's legal claim against the employer for damages.

12.12 FIRST AID

Employers must ensure that there are adequate first aid provisions for their employees. This will depend on:

- The size of the business.
- The nature of the work.
- The employer's resources.
- Location of the workplace.
- Number of employees.

First aid boxes, and where appropriate travelling first aid kits, must be made available. 'Suitable persons' must be provided by the employer to administer first aid in an emergency. A 'suitable person' is deemed to be:

- A person who holds a current first aid certificate issued by a Health and Safety Executive (HSE) approved organisation.
- Any other properly trained and/or qualified person approved by the HSE.

As a guideline, during normal working hours, the employer should provide at least one first aider for every 50 employees. In hazardous work environments this ratio should be increased. Information in respect of first aid arrangements should be conspicuously displayed in the workplace, providing names of first aiders and the location of equipment.

12.13 DANGEROUS SUBSTANCES

Regulations exist controlling substances classified as hazardous to health. The employer must assess the risks associated with hazardous substances in the workplace and take steps to eliminate or control those risks. The regulations apply to:

- Substances which are listed as toxic, very toxic, harmful, irritant or corrosive.
- Substances with maximum occupational exposure limits.
- Harmful micro-organisms.
- Substantial quantities of dust.
- Other substances which create a comparable hazard to the health of an employee.

The employer must take all reasonable steps to limit exposure to such substances, to provide protective equipment and/or clothing and to monitor the hazardous substances. They must also provide their employees with adequate information, instruction and training in order for them to take appropriate precautions and limit their exposure to the substance.

12.14 NOISE

In a working environment where the daily noise exposure is no less than 85 db (A), the employer must assess the noise level and inform all employees if ear protection is required and, if so, provide adequate ear protection. Furthermore, the employer must do all reasonably within their capability to limit or reduce noise at the place of work. However, employers are under no legal duty to require employees to take regular hearing tests.

12.15 VISUAL DISPLAY UNITS

It is now quite common in an office environment for many employees to have on their desks a VDU or other display screen equipment (DSE). Health hazards are caused by the long use and exposure to such apparatus. Regulations now exist requiring employers to take steps to protect the health and safety of VDU/DSE users. Workstations must be assessed to establish whether any risk to health exists, particularly in respect of stress and fatigue. Equipment must be:

- Adjustable.
- Glare free.
- Appropriately lit.
- Maintained at an appropriate temperature.

Where an employer works for many hours before DSE, regular work breaks or changes in activity must be provided. DSE users are entitled to appropriate eyesight tests that must be paid for by the employer. Should spectacles be prescribed to correct vision defects as a result of DSE work, the cost of such spectacles must be borne by the employer. Over use of DSE can lead to:

- Eye strain.
- Headaches.
- Stress.
- Limb strain.
- Dermatitis (facial).
- Epileptic fits.

Compliance with the regulations is designed to combat these complaints.

12.16 LIFTING AND CARRYING

Manual Handling Operations Regulations exist to ensure that injury sustained through lifting and carrying at the workplace is controlled and the prospect of injury minimised. The regulations require assessment of the risks by the employer with a view to making sensible procedural changes if required. Consideration must be given to the capabilities of the employees involved in such activity and they must be trained to handle and move heavy loads safely. Where appropriate, moving or lifting equipment should be provided for the employees.

12.17 MACHINERY

Machines, whether manual or automated, present an obvious hazard in the workplace. Statutory requirements in respect of new equipment are in place which ensure:

- The adequate maintenance of machinery.
- Its suitability for the job.
- The provision of information about its use by the employee.
- Instruction for use.
- Training for use.
- European standard conformity.

For existing equipment as at January 1st 1997 further requirements are in force covering:

- Dangerous parts of machinery.
- Protection against specific hazards.
- Temperature extremes.
- Control systems.
- Power isolation.
- Stability.
- Lighting.
- Markings and warnings.

The purpose of these regulated matters is to provide the employee with a safer working environment where it involves the use of machinery in the performance of their duties.

12.18 FIRE

Employers are under a duty to minimise the risk of fire, and to inform the employees as to:

- Escape routes.
- Fire drill.
- The use of extinguishers/fire blankets where appropriate.
- Precautionary measures.
- Warning systems.

All employees should be clearly aware of the procedures to be adopted at their place of work in the event of a fire and of the need generally to prevent it, how to prevent its spread and the importance of keeping fire exit points free from obstacles.

12.19 MAINTAINING THE WORKPLACE

Maintaining the workplace has often been described as 'good housekeeping' measures. In fact, the regulations currently in force place specific duties and obligations on the employer and any breach which adversely effects the well-being of an employee may lead to a legitimate claim for damages. Regulations exist in respect of the following matters:

- Workplace, equipment and work systems maintenance.
- Ventilation.
- Workplace temperature.
- Lighting.
- Cleanliness.
- Room dimensions of the workplace.
- Floor condition.
- Traffic routes.
- Falling objects.
- Windows, doors, gates, walls, skylights, ventilators.
- Lifts and moving walkways.
- Sanitation.
- Toilets.
- Washing facilities.
- Drinking water.
- Accommodation for clothing, changing and eating meals.
- Rest room accommodation for non-smokers.

12.20 THE HEALTH AND SAFETY EXECUTIVE (HSE)

The HSE has overall responsibility for enforcing the existing health and safety laws and regulations and is the main enforcing authority. In respect of certain workplaces and premises the local authority also has powers of enforcement. For example:

- Offices.
- Shops.
- Public houses.
- Sports centres.
- Restaurants.

An HSE inspector is empowered to enter premises with or without a police officer for the purpose of inspection, examination or investigation. They may take with them equipment to assist them in their purpose and take samples of anything found on the premises. Further to their investigations they may interview representatives of the employer and employees without interference. Upon the recommendations of the inspector's report the HSE may order an improvement or prohibition notice.

12.20.1 IMPROVEMENT NOTICE

This may be issued where the employer:

- Is contravening one or more statutory provision; or
- Has contravened such provisions in circumstances where it is likely that contravention will continue.

The improvement notice requires the contravention to be remedied within a specified period of time of not less than 21 days.

12.20.2 PROHIBITION NOTICE

The notice must:

- State the inspector's belief regarding the risk of serious personal injury.
- Specify what is responsible for the risk.
- State the inspector's belief that an actual or potential breach of a statutory provision is involved.
- Direct that the unsafe practice or activity must not continue.

12.21 PROSECUTION

In certain circumstances, the employer's actions are such that criminal proceedings may be issued against them. Generally such action would be considered by the HSE where the employer has:

- Failed to discharge a general duty under the statutory Health and Safety provisions.
- Breached Health and Safety regulations.
- Made a false statement or entry in a register, document etc. required to be kept by law.
- Failed to comply with an improvement or prohibition notice.
- Obstructed an inspector in the course of their duty.

Where the employer is a limited company, it is possible in law for criminal proceedings to be brought against a specific director or officer of that company where the breach is committed with the consent, connivance or neglect of that person. Such proceedings are rare. Summary proceedings before a magistrates court must be brought within 6 months from the date upon which it was known by the enforcing authority that a breach of the statutory regulations had been committed. Penalties include fines and/or imprisonment.

12.21.1 EMPLOYER'S DEFENCE

A common thread runs through most of the statutory provisions relating to the health and safety of employee at the workplace. That is, employers are obliged to act under the regulations in so far as is reasonably practicable given the circumstances of the case. It follows that a defence is provided in law for the employer where they can show that such an obligation has been discharged.

12.22 UNFAIR DISMISSAL AND HEALTH AND SAFETY

This is dealt with in section 4.4.6.

12.23 WORKING HOURS AND REST BREAKS

Long hours and lapses in concentration can cause serious injury and in some cases can be fatal. To combat this the Working Time Regulations were introduced into the United Kingdom in 1998. The provisions currently apply to all categories of workers except workers employed in the following sectors:

- Air transport.
- Rail transport.
- Road transport.
- Sea transport.
- Inland waterways and lake transport.
- Sea fishing.
- Other work at sea.
- Doctors in training.
- Armed forces.
- Police.
- Civil protection services.
- Domestic servants in private households.

The reason for the transport industry exclusion is that alternative provisions protect employees against long continuous hours of work, for example, tachograph regulations.

12.23.1 48 HOUR WEEK

All workers under a contract of employment (including agency workers), other than those specified above, are, from 1st October 1998, subject to a maximum working week not exceeding 48 hours. Employees may modify the effect of this regulation by devising a collective agreement with trades unions or a workforce agreement extending the reference period from 17 weeks to 52 weeks. The reference period is the time span over which the hourly week is calculated and, unless modified, must be 17 weeks. However, workers and employers can enter into individual voluntary agreements to disapply the 48 hour maximum. Agreements must be in writing and should have a notice of termination clause not exceeding 3 months. On call at home will not generally constitute working time.

12.23.2 REST BREAKS

Adult employees (18 years of age or over) are entitled to 11 hours rest in every 24 hour working period. They are also entitled to not less than 24 hours rest in each 7 day period or 48 hours rest in each 14 day period. The employer may decide which of these to apply. Employees are also entitled to 20 minutes rest break during the working day where daily working time is more than 6 hours. These rest breaks must be uninterrupted.

Young workers (over minimum school leaving age but under 18 years of age) are entitled to 12 hours rest in any 24 hour working period, 48 hours rest (starting from midnight) in each 7 day working period and 30 minutes rest break during the working day where daily working time is more than 4.5 hours. Again, these rest breaks must be uninterrupted. Young workers' weekly rest period of 48 hours in each 7 day period may be reduced to 36 hours if justified by technical or organisational reasons.

Breaks are unpaid and can be modified or excluded by collective or workforce agreement subject to the employee being permitted to take an equivalent period of compensatory rest (see section 12.23.4). Where work is of a monotonous nature or hazardous to health, the employer must ensure adequate breaks are taken.

12.23.3 NIGHT WORKERS

The regulations state maximum hours. Any employee who works at least 3 hours of their daily working time during the hours of 11pm and 6am is a night worker. Workforce, collective or individual agreements may be drafted to include a night period different to that specified, but the period must be of at least 7 hours which must include midnight to 5am. Employers are required to take all reasonable steps to ensure that night workers (unless they fall within an exempt category or derogation) do not work more than an average of 8 hours in any 24 hour period. There is a reference period of 17 weeks to calculate the number of hours worked. Unless modified, Health and Safety bodies can use a snapshot of any 17 week period during the working year to calculate hours worked. All night workers are entitled to a free health assessment before starting night work and at regular intervals thereafter. This can be done by the completion of an initial health questionnaire then referral to a doctor if necessary. A night worker is entitled to be transferred to day work on request if they have medical evidence indicating that night working is affecting their health. They are not entitled to transfer with any enhancements such as extra pay. The employer is not required to dismiss a day worker to make room for such a transfer but is required to reassign workers, if possible, subject to their agreement. Employers must not contract out of the right to health assessment or transfer.

12.23.4 DEROGATIONS/EXCEPTIONS

Unmeasured Working Time

This covers workers whose time cannot be measured or predetermined and covers managing executives, family workers, workers officiating at religious ceremonies in churches and religious communities. Such workers are not subject to regulations governing a 48 hour week, length of night work or rest breaks.

Work Specific Activities

Includes security and surveillance workers and 24 hour service providers, e.g. dockers, medical workers, hotel staff, postal workers, farmers, tourism workers, refuse collectors, gas, water and electricity providers. Regulations relating to night work and breaks do not apply.

NB. Although exempt, these workers are entitled to compensatory rest, which constitutes a rest period equivalent to that specified in the regulations to be taken at times other than those specified in the regulations.

Shift Workers

These are workers whose work schedule is part of shift work, whereby each worker replaces another at the same continuous work station, e.g. factory machine workers. Such workers are exempt from the rest break provisions.

NB. Although exempt, these workers are entitled to compensatory rest, which constitutes a rest period equivalent to that specified in the regulations to be taken at times other than those specified in the regulations. The employer must observe the entitlement to compensatory rest.

The above derogations are subject to any relevant Health and Safety Regulations.

12.23.5 ENFORCEMENT

Employment tribunals will enforce rest breaks, annual leave and compensatory rest. Claims must be brought within 3 months of the act complained of and, if successful, awards of compensation may be made. The employer must not subject employees to any detriment as a result of the rights and obligations arising under the regulations; such treatment would give rise to a claim. It is also automatically unfair dismissal to dismiss an employee for a reason related to the regulations, irrespective of their length of service. Health and Safety bodies will enforce the maximum working week, maximum night work, and duty to provide health assessment.

Sanctions include criminal penalties such as conviction, fine and imprisonment. Health and Safety bodies have the right of access to information and records. If an employer fails to comply, criminal sanctions are available. Employers must keep proper written records of night workers, all hours worked, compensatory rest periods, work patterns and leave.

12.23.6 WORKFORCE AGREEMENTS

These Agreements must be in writing and specify the start date and only apply to relevant members of the workforce. To be valid, they must be signed prior to the start date by the majority of those who are relevant members of the workforce (only if there are 20 or fewer workers employed by the employer) or by elected representatives. These representatives must be elected by secret ballot. The employer is free to determine the number of representatives to be elected and the term for which they are elected. All members of the workforce are eligible to stand as candidates and all of them are entitled to vote. To be valid, the workforce must have seen copies of the agreement prior to signature together with guidance to assist their understanding. The agreement must have effect for no more than 5 years.

12.23.7 INDIVIDUAL AGREEMENTS

These are agreements entered into voluntarily by the employee and employer. They must be in writing, e.g. to work in excess of the weekly working time limit.

12.23.8 COLLECTIVE AGREEMENTS

These are agreements reached between an employer and a trade union recognised by that employer for collective bargaining purposes. They do not have to be in writing but to be enforceable they must be incorporated into the contract of employment either by reference or expressly.

12.24 CASE STUDY

Kevin works for Keith's photo-copier leasing company 'Copymagic'. Kevin sells photo-copy paper to Copymagic clients and his sales area is extensive covering the whole of the south coast of England from Cornwall to Rochester. As a result, Kevin works very long hours travelling considerable distances each day between clients in his area in the execution of his duties.

Since commencing employment with Keith, Kevin's circumstances have changed. His wife has given birth to their first child, Esmerelda. Due to family commitments Kevin no longer wishes to work the 60 hours a week he has worked in practice over the last 3 years. Kevin would like to reduce his hours. He has approached Keith about the matter but Keith is unsympathetic and points to a clause in Kevin's contract of employment that states:

"You will work such hours as are necessary for the better performance of your duties as a Copymagic sales person".

Kevin is desperate to spend more time with Esmerelda and his wife. He seeks legal advice.

Taking a reference period of 17 weeks, Kevin works, on average, more than 48 hours per week. Kevin may, with immediate effect, legitimately refuse to work more than 48 hours per week — on average. This is a statutory right and as such overrides any provision to the contrary within his contract of employment with Copymagic. However, if Keith dismisses Kevin for asserting his statutory right or imposes any other detriment, Kevin may claim unfair dismissal and/or compensation (whichever is appropriate), provided he brings his claim before an employment tribunal within 3 months of the act complained of. Travel that is required by the job counts as working time.

CHAPTER THIRTEEN
MISCELLANEOUS

13.1 INTRODUCTION

There are a number of aspects of employment law about which an employee should know. Often they do not fit neatly into a wider area of employment law even though individually they may be of considerable importance and touch the working lives of many people. The purpose of this final chapter is to address the main miscellaneous areas of employment law not detailed in previous sections of this book but are nonetheless worthy of note. The following sections are expressed in no particular order of importance.

13.2 REFERENCES

Contrary to popular belief, an employee in the UK has no legal entitlement to a reference from their previous employer, even where failure to provide a reference will almost surely lose the applicant the opportunity of employment with a prospective employer.

Should an ex-employer provide a reference whether orally (over the telephone) or in writing for a prospective employer it must be accurate and the person giving the reference must believe its content to be true. If it is inaccurate and a lie, particularly if driven by spite or malice it could well be defamatory allowing the employee a right to claim damages for libel (if in writing) or slander (if oral). However, before considering such an action against an ex-employer, the individual would need good evidence and be aware that such actions are notoriously costly and not subject to the assistance of legal aid.

The courts have recently suggested that it will be unlawful discrimination for an employer to fail to provide a reference on grounds of sex, race or disability. Notwithstanding that at the time of alleging discrimination as the motive for failing to provide a reference, the individual will no longer be the employee of the alleged discrimanator.

There is one further consideration on the matter of references and that is their position in relation to a settlement. Often following the termination of employment, there is a dispute between the employer and ex-employee. In most cases an amicable settlement is achieved. An agreed reference can become an important aspect of the settlement and ex-employees in that situation would be well advised to be fully aware of the commercial value of a good reference. An extra £500 on a sum in settlement may appear attractive, but what price a reference which may secure further employment?

13.3 ACCESS TO MEDICAL REPORTS

Often, when an employee has been off work, injured or ill, for some time an employer will seek to assess the situation by requesting a medical report either from the employees own doctor or an independent consultant. Under The Access To Medical Reports Act 1988 the employee has the right to access to any such medical report before the employer has sight of the report.

A medical report for the purposes of the Act includes any report relating to the physical or mental condition of its subject. It covers reports compiled by the employees own doctor, any consultant or company appointed doctor. The employer must not approach the employee's doctor without the employee's permission in writing. The employer's request for permission to approach the doctor for a medical report must also state the employee's right to:

- Withhold consent.
- Demand access to the report before it is sent to the employer.
- Access to the report after it has been delivered to the employer.
- Ask that the report be amended.
- Refuse to allow the report to be sent to the employer.

Under the rules of access, the employee is entitled to a copy of the report or to sight of the original. The employee's right to make amendments to the report exists where they believe any part of it is incorrect or misleading. The employee may request that the doctor makes changes to the report. If the doctor agrees to the changes, it is amended before being sent to the employer. If the doctor refuses to make changes the employee cannot insist that they are made. Instead a copy of the employee's objections is attached to the report before it is sent to the employer. There are situations where the doctor need not give the employee access to the whole or part of the medical report. This occurs where disclosure would:

- In the doctor's opinion, be likely to cause serious harm to the physical or mental health of the employee or anyone else.
- Indicate the doctor's intentions in respect of the individual.
- Be likely to reveal information about another person.
- Be likely to reveal the identity of another person who has supplied the doctor with information in respect of the employee.

If the doctor seeks to rely on any of the exemptions they must notify the employee accordingly. Should any of the provisions of the Act not be complied with by the employer or the doctor, the employee may complain upon application to the county court which is empowered to order compliance.

More generally, the Access To Health Records Act 1990 allows an employee or any individual to request in writing access to their health record or any part of it from a doctor including a company doctor. Where this request is made within 40 days from the date on which the record was made, the record must be produced within 21 days of the request without charge. Where the record is more than 40 days old, a charge (currently £10) may be levied. The cost of copying and posting may also be charged. The right to access to health records does not apply to any records made before November 1 1991. Moreover, for those records made after that date there exist exclusions where:

- To provide access could cause harm to the physical or mental health of the patient.
- Another individual could be identified by the information (excluding health care professionals).

13.4 REHABILITATION OF OFFENDERS AND EMPLOYMENT

The Rehabilitation Of Offenders Act 1974 provides that after a set period of time those individuals who have committed certain criminal offences are entitled to regard the conviction as spent. The meaning of 'spent' is taken as regarding the offence as not having been committed when in certain circumstances a person is asked about their criminal record.

Within an employment environment, job applicants are often asked at interview or within an application form whether they have any criminal convictions. Provided the conviction is spent, subject to certain excluded professions, the employee is under no duty to disclose the conviction if asked. Failure to disclose a spent conviction is not dishonest, it is acting in compliance with the law.

An employer may not dismiss an employee merely because they discover that the employee has a spent conviction. People in certain occupations and professions are obliged to disclose spent convictions and may be dismissed or excluded from employment because of the conviction. These occupations are:

- Doctors.
- Nurses.
- Midwives.
- Dentists.
- Barristers.
- Solicitors.
- Accountants.
- Judges.
- Teachers.
- Police officers.
- Directors and Officers of Building Societies.
- Those who have access to children in the normal course of duties.
- Veterinary Surgeons.
- Opticians.
- Chemists.
- Traffic Wardens.
- Firearms dealers.
- Probation officers.
- Prison officers.
- Securities Dealers.

13.4.1 THE REHABILITATION PERIODS

SENTENCE	PERIOD BEFORE CONVICTION IS SPENT
Life imprisonment	Never
Imprisonment for 30 months or more	Never
Imprisonment for a period between 6 months and 30 months	10 years
Imprisonment for 6 months or less	7 years
A criminal fine	5 years
Detention of a child or young person between 6 months and 30 months	5 years
Detention of a child or young person for 6 months or less	3 years
Conditional discharge, probation, care or supervision order, a bind-over to keep the peace	1 year or the duration of the order, whichever is the longer
Disqualification from driving	The length of disqualification but where there is a fine, 5 years
Absolute discharge	6 months
A criminal fine for a child or young person	2½ years

13.5 THE EMPLOYMENT OF CHILDREN

The employment of children is governed by legislation. There are a number of restrictions which must be complied with when considering employing a child. For these purposes, a child is a person who has not yet attained minimum school leaving age. In England and Wales, a child can leave school on the last Friday in June if they are 16 or will be 16 before the start of the next school year.

The restrictions

The main provisions which restrict the employment of children are set out below. As a general rule, a child may not be employed (whether the work is paid or unpaid):

- If he is under the age of 14 years; or
- To do any work other than light work; or
- During school hours on any school day; or
- Before 7 am or after 7pm on any day; or
- For more than 2 hours on any school day; or
- For more than 2 hours on any Sunday; or
- For more than 8 hours (or if he is aged under 15 years, for more than 5 hours) on any Saturday or any other day on which he is not required to attend school (other than Sundays); or
- For more than 35 hours (or if he is aged under 15 years, for more than 25 hours) in any week in which he is not required to attend school; or
- For more than 4 hours in any day without a rest break of at least 1 hour; or
- At any time in a year unless he has had or could still have at least 2 consecutive weeks off during a school holiday.

Failure to comply with any of the restrictions set out above may lead to criminal prosecution and the imposition of a fine of up to £1,000.

What is light work?

Light work means work which is not likely to be harmful to the child's health, safety, development, attendance at school or participation in work experience. A health and safety risk assessment must also be carried out and information on the outcome provided to the child's parents. The employment of children is prohibited for work:

- Which is beyond their physical or psychological capacity;
- Which involves harmful exposure to toxic or carcinogenic agents or agents which cause heritable genetic damage or harm to the unborn child or which in any other way chronically affect human health;
- Which involves harmful exposure to radiation;
- Which involves the risk of accidents which it may reasonably be assumed cannot be appreciated or avoided by a child owing to his insufficient attention to safety or lack of experience; or

- In which there is a risk to health from extreme cold, heat, noise or vibration.

In addition, no child can be employed in any industrial undertaking, i.e. mines, quarries, factories, building and works of engineering construction and transportation.

Powers of the local authority

In addition to the restrictions set out above, local authorities have the power to pass bye-laws restricting the employment of children. For example, any bye-laws may authorise the employment of children under the age of 14 years by their parents or guardians in light agricultural or horticultural work, or may authorise the employment of children aged 13 years in certain categories of light work as specified in the bye-law. Since each local authority has its own powers, it is important that employers check with their local education authority to see whether there are any bye-laws of which they need to be aware.

Note, that breach of a bye-law is a criminal offence and again the fine of up to £1,000 will apply.

Requirement for work permit

Each local authority generally has the power to supervise the employment of children in its geographical area. Many local authorities require the employer to obtain a work permit enabling the child to carry out the particular work. In summary, the local authority may require details of how the child is employed and at what times and for what periods before a permit is granted.

13.5.1 WORK EXPERIENCE

The rules above are relaxed where the child is in their last academic year of schooling and the job is for work experience and the arrangements for such employment are made or approved by the local education authority.

13.5.2 YOUNG PERSONS

A 'young-person' is defined as an individual who is no longer a child (above school leaving age) but who is under the age of 18. Generally, there are few restrictions on the employment of young persons whether in offices, shops or factories. Many of the restrictions have been repealed as recently as 1989.

There is one important aspect of the employment of young persons that should not be overlooked – an exception to a general legal rule. In nearly all other areas of law, a person under the age of 18 is deemed a minor and therefore not able to enter into a legally binding contract. Employment contracts for young persons between school leaving age and 18 are an exception. Such contracts, provided freely entered into, are binding and enforceable in law should the young employee be in breach of its terms and conditions. Apprenticeship agreements are similarly regarded.

13.6 SERVICE LETTINGS

There are a number of industries, for example in catering, within which it is common to offer a person a residence along with the job. Difficulties can arise when the employment comes to an end. Generally, an ex-employee will only retain the right to continue residing in the employer's premises if the occupancy amounts to a separate tenancy. A service occupier in law never becomes a tenant and the employer never becomes a landlord. The relationship remains one of master and servant, that is, one of employment.

In most cases the right to reside in any particular premises as part of the job offer, is clearly stated within the contract of employment. Where it is so stated there can be no confusion and no creation of a separate tenancy. The circumstances of employment and residence may also imply a relationship that creates a service letting and not a tenancy. The facts of each particular case must be assessed on their own merits. Where there is no express statement of a service letting but it is clear the accommodation was offered for the better or more effective performance of an employee's duties it is very likely to be regarded by the courts as a service letting.

13.6.1 TERMINATION OF EMPLOYMENT – IMPLICATIONS FOR SERVICE LETTINGS

If the contract of employment is brought to an end by whatever reason under a service letting, the employee's contractual right to occupy the property ceases. Usually the employer will provide a reasonable period of time within which the property must be vacated by the ex-employee, for example 28 days. If the ex-employee remains in the property after such time they will be acting unlawfully and the employer may seek a court order for possession of the property. Should the employer seek to evict the ex-employee forcibly or in any other way harass the ex-employee, this may constitute a criminal offence and the police should be informed.

Ex-employees in this situation should be aware that if the employer has good grounds for possession of a true service letting and seeks a court order to that effect, they may also claim damages based on the unlawful possession of the property by the ex-employee from the point in time when they no longer had the right of residence. These damages will be based on the reasonable rent which could have been taken for the property in question and could be considerable by the time the court orders possession in favour of the employer. For an employer to seek an order for possession they must show that:

- The property was occupied by the employee for the term of employment and for the better and more effective performance of their duties.
- The contract of employment has been effectively terminated.
- Reasonable or proper notice for possession has been given to the ex-employee.

- No new tenancy arrangement has been created between the parties.

13.7 RESTRAINT OF TRADE

It is now quite common for a contract of employment to contain clauses that seek to restrain the employee in some way after the contract has been terminated. These clauses are sometimes referred to as restrictive covenants – the two terms are interchangeable. Such clauses are included to restrict many activities most typically:

- Working for a competitor.
- Working in the same industry.
- The soliciting of the ex-employer's clients or customers.
- The soliciting of the ex-employer's staff.
- Breach of confidentiality.
- The passing of trade secrets.

For the court to uphold such clauses against the employee it is essential that two conditions are fulfilled, the nature of the restraint must be reasonable:

- Between the parties.
- In the public interest.

In essence, employers must only use these clauses to protect legitimate business interests. They will not be upheld if they are intended to punish the employee for leaving the employer and act to prevent the ex-employee from earning a living in the only business they know. A balance has to be achieved between these two competing interests. The main points to remember in respect of restraint of trade clauses are:

- They are unlikely to be enforceable if they are drafted in vague or uncertain terms.
- Some attempt must be made to define the geographical area of restraint and the time limit within which activity is restricted.
- The clause must be reasonable and not punitive.
- The question of reasonableness is ultimately one for the courts.
- Any definitions within the clauses must be certain and clear.
- The courts will not re-write badly drafted clauses in order to make them effective and enforceable.
- They must be no greater than is necessary to protect legitimate business interests.
- Restraint of trade clauses will be examined in their context, each profession, trade or industry will have different levels of acceptability.
- If an employer dismisses an employee wrongfully (in breach of contract), normally they will be prevented from seeking to impose any restraint of trade clause that exists within the contract of employment.

- Employers can legitimately protect only the following:

1. Trade secrets.
2. Confidential information.
3. Trade connections.
4. Goodwill.
5. Existing staff.

The following will always be considered by the court:

- The nature of the employer's business.
- The scope of their business.
- The geographical area of intended restraint.
- The duration in time of the intended restraint.
- The status and responsibilities of the employee.

Should the clause not offend any of these 'rules' the employer may enforce its terms against an employee in breach, by seeking an injunction in the county court to restrain the employee from continuing their activities. The employer may also claim damages where the financial loss to his business is quantifiable.

13.8 SEASONAL EMPLOYEES

Those individuals who work for a limited period of time, for example a summer or winter season, are nonetheless regarded as employees by the law. Most, by the nature of their short period of work, will not secure the right to claim unfair dismissal or a statutory redundancy payment upon termination of the contract of employment. However, many will work for 4 weeks or more and therefore be entitled to a statement of written particulars of employment. All will be entitled to the statutory minimum period of notice on termination.

In certain situations, particularly where the employee concerned is habitually re-engaged time and time again by the same employer, the employee may retain continuity of service between each period of work. This is possible where the period without work is regarded in law as a temporary cessation of work. Where this is so, full employment rights may accrue after one years' service with the same employer. As with all employment law, each case must be assessed on its own particular facts and circumstances.

13.9 FIXED-TERM CONTRACTS

Increasingly, employers are placing employees on fixed-term contracts. There are two main reasons for this occurrence:

1. A properly formalised fixed-term contract can be a convenient method for the employer to avoid liability for statutory redundancy payments after 2 years continuous service.
2. Such contracts can 'bind' a key-employee into the business.

The definition of a fixed-term contract is one which has a specific beginning and end. Usually characterised by the phrase,

...”you will be employed with effect from (date) and continue in employment until (date).”

The law allows an employer who is entering into a fixed-term contract to include a waiver clause which operates expressly to exclude the employee from claiming statutory redundancy pay at the expiry of the contract. For this exclusion to be binding the contract must be for a minimum period of 2 years.

In addition, the waiver clause will only be effective if the contract is properly drafted and formalised. In practice, there is one consistently repeated error by many employers which undermines the effectiveness of an otherwise simple waiver procedure. The problem occurs where a fixed-term contract is 'renewed' by the employer. All too often, due formality is not present upon renewal and the employee is merely told (orally or in writing) that the fixed-term contract is extended for a further defined period and the terms of the original fixed-term contract are to be viewed as continuing.

The law quite clearly states that for the waiver to be effective there must be a new waiver (signed and agreed by the employee) in respect of each contract. Failure to meet this requirement can be used to the employee's advantage since it will expose the employer to unfair dismissal and redundancy rights where there exists appropriate continuous service.

Should the employee be dismissed within the defined period of the contract for no valid reason, they may bring a claim for damages in respect of breach of contract against the employer. Damages are based on what the employee would have earned over the remaining period of the fixed-term. The employee will always be under a duty to mitigate their loss and actively seek comparable work. This may act to reduce the amount claimed.

ACAS. Advisory, Conciliation and Arbitration Service.

Accrued Holiday Entitlement. 'Earned' holiday untaken.

Action. A case brought before a court or tribunal.

Adjournment. The postponement of a court case to a later date.

Appeal. The act of challenging the decision of an employer or court by taking the matter before another decision-making panel or higher court in the hope that the original decision will be overturned or otherwise altered.

Applicant. The employee bringing the action against the employer before an industrial tribunal.

Attachment of Earnings Order. Having obtained judgment, the creditor can use this to deduct a percentage of the debtor's wages for a certain time period or until the judgment is paid off.

Bank Holiday. A statutory holiday, for example; Christmas Day, Boxing Day, Good Friday etc.

Bankrupt. A person who has had a bankruptcy order made against them for the benefit of the bankrupt's creditors.

Bankruptcy. The process by which an insolvent individual is made bankrupt and their assets administered for the benefit of their creditors.

Cashless Pay. A method of payment e.g. cheque, bank credit, other than by cash.

Casual Worker. A worker employed for a short period of time or for a series of short periods in accordance with the work flow of the employer.

Claimant. Claiming party in a law-suit. The modern term for Plaintiff.

Closed-shop. The situation where a person may not be employed by a certain employer unless they are a member of a particular trade union.

Code of Practice. A set of rules which are not legally binding.

Collective Bargaining. Where trade unions negotiate terms on behalf of their members with employers.

Compromise Agreement. A formal and legally binding written agreement between the employer and employee, to terminate the contract of employment.

Consideration. Pay.

Constructive Dismissal. The situation whereby an employee, through the unreasonable actions of their employer, is entitled to regard themselves as having been dismissed.

Contract. A legally binding agreement made either orally or in writing which usually has the three ingredients: parties, price, performance.

Contracting-out. Where an employer, rather than using existing staff uses the services of an outside contractor to undertake specific tasks.

Contributory Fault/Negligence. The amount of blame for which the party bringing the action is adjudged to be responsible.

Counter-claim. A 'cross' action which is not a defence, which allows the defendant in the original proceedings to make a claim against the person suing him.

County Court. The 'lowest' civil court in England and Wales with the jurisdiction over civil actions up to a financial limit.

CRE. Commission For Racial Equality.

Cross-examination. When a witness has been intentionally called by either party, the opposite party has a right to cross-examine him. Failure to cross-examine generally leads to the witness' version of events being accepted.

Damages. A court's estimated compensation in money terms for a wrong suffered in contract or other disputes.

Defendant. The individual who is being sued.

Disciplinary Hearing. The forum by which it may be established whether or not an employee has committed an act of misconduct.

DRC. Disability Rights Commission.

DSE. Display Screen Equipment.

DSS. The Department of Social Security.

EC-country. European Community – country.

EDT. Effective Date of Termination of the contract of employment.

Employers Liability Insurance. Compulsory insurance required by employers in the event of an employee being injured whilst in the course of their duties.

Employment Tribunal. The employment 'court' in which disputes between employers and employees may be heard.

EOC. Equal Opportunities Commission.

ETO. In matters relating to the transfer of a business, the employer may defend a claim for unfair dismissal where they can show the termination to be necessary by Economic, Technical or Organisational reason.

EWC. In respect of maternity matters – the Expected Week of Confinement.

Family Emergency. The statutory definition of a set of circumstances in which an employee is entitled to immediate unpaid leave to address the emergency.

Fixed-term Contract. A contract of employment that by prior agreement between the parties is set to run for a finite period of time (e.g. 2 years).

Gross Misconduct. An act so serious that the contract of employment, from that point onwards, may be regarded by the employer as being at an end.

High Court. Superior to the county court with no financial limit to its jurisdiction.

House of Lords. The highest court in the United Kingdom.

HSE. Health And Safety Executive.

Indemnity. Compensate.

Industrial Action. Action taken by employees against their employer in furtherance of a dispute between them.

Injunction. An order granted by a court preventing an individual or employer from doing a particular thing.

'In Lieu'. 'Instead of'.

Insolvent. Of a company or individual – unable to pay debts.

Judgment. The decision of the court in a matter before it.

Jurisdiction. Whether the court or tribunal has the power or ability to hear a particular dispute.

Lay-off. A period during a contract of employment, without work.

Legislation. Law enacted by Parliament.

MA. Maternity Allowance.

Mitigation. The process by which a person or business may reduce the amount of damages to be awarded in their favour.

'Moonlighting'. Undertaking work in addition to a main contract of employment.

MPP. The Maternity Pay Period.

NMW. The National Minimum Wage.

Notice of Appearance. Employer's defence submitted to the employment tribunal.

Originating Application. Employee's claim submitted to an employment tribunal.

Parental Leave. The statutory entitlement of all parents to unpaid leave in the first few years of their child's life.

Part-time Worker. A worker who works only part of a normal working week.

Paternity Leave. A father's right to leave following the birth of his child.

Piece-work. A method of payment relating to the production of items by the employee.

PIW. In respect of statutory sick pay – a period of incapacity for work.

Quantum. The amount of money sought or payable for damages.

QW. In respect of maternity rights – the Qualifying Week.

Respondent. The employer being sued before an industrial tribunal.

Restraint of Trade. See Restrictive Covenant.

Restrictive Covenant. The means by which an employer may restrain an employee from working after the contract of employment has ended.

Seasonal Worker. A worker employed for only a part of the year e.g. during peak season.

Short-time Work. Work which is less than a full working week.

SMP. Statutory Maternity Pay.

SSP. Statutory Sick Pay.

Standard of Proof. The amount of proof required before an individual or employer may be deemed to be liable for a particular act.

Statutory Guarantee Payment. The amount paid by the state to all employees affected by lay-off or short-time working.

Statutory Right. A 'right' provided under an Act of Parliament.

Sue. The process of bringing a civil action in the court or tribunal.

Summary Judgment. Judgment granted by the court without the need for a full hearing.

Trade Union Ballot. The official method of voting by trade union members.

Transfer of an Undertaking. The sale or passing of a business from one person, or company, to another.

TUPE. Transfer of Undertakings (Protection of Employment) Regulations 1981.

Union Recognition. Where an employer officially recognises a trade union(s) for the purpose of collective negotiations.

Unlawful Deduction. A deduction from wages made without the prior written consent of the employee.

VDU. Visual Display Unit.

Working Time Regulations (WTR). Statutory regulations controlling hours worked, holiday entitlement, night work, rest periods etc.

There exist a great number of text books on employment law aimed at employment lawyers and personnel professionals. Many of these books express the law in comprehensive detail and may be a useful source of reference for a particularly complex issue. The following are sources for such detailed information:

Grunfeld, The Law Of Redundancy, Third Edition,
(Sweet and Maxwell)

Harvey, On Industrial Relations And Employment Law,
(Butterworths)

IDS Employment Law Handbooks (on a wide-range of issues),
(Incomes Data Services Ltd.)

Selwyn, The Law Of Health And Safety At Work – 1998/99,
(Croner Publications)

Tolley's, Employment Handbook, Thirteenth Edition,
(Tolley Publishing Co. Ltd.)

The Law Of Termination Of Employment, Fourth Edition,
(Sweet and Maxwell)

The Offices Of The Advisory Conciliation And Arbitration Service (ACAS)

HEAD OFFICE
27 Wilton Street, London
SW1X 7AZ.
Tel: 020 7 3965100

NORTHERN REGION
Westgate House, Westgate
Road, Newcastle upon Tyne
NE1 1TJ.
Tel: 0191 261 2191

Cumbria, Tyne and Wear,
Cleveland, Northumberland
Durham

YORKSHIRE AND HUMBERSIDE REGION
Commerce House,
St. Albans Place, Leeds
LS2 8HH.
Tel: 01132 431371

North Yorkshire, South
Yorkshire, Humberside,
West Yorkshire

LONDON REGION
Clifton House,
83-117 Euston Road,
London NW1 2RB.
Tel: 020 7 396 5100

Greater London

Note: A direct line is available
in the London region for use in
cases where a request is being
made for conciliation services
before a complaint is made to
an industrial tribunal. The
number is: 020 7 396 5150

SOUTH EAST REGION
Westminster House,

125 Fleet Road, Fleet
GU13 8PD.
Tel: 01252 811868

Cambridgeshire, Bedfordshire,
Hampshire *(except Ringwood)*,
Norfolk, Hertfordshire, Isle of
Wight, Suffolk, Essex, East
Sussex, Oxfordshire, Berkshire,
West Sussex, Buckinghamshire,
Surrey, Kent

SOUTH WEST REGION
Regent House,
27a Regent Street, Clifton,
Bristol BS8 4HR.
Tel: 01179 469500

Gloucestershire, Cornwall,
Dorset, Avon, Devon,
Ringwood, Wiltshire, Somerset

MIDLANDS REGION
Leonard House,
319-323 Bradford Street,
Birmingham B5 6ET.
Tel: 0121 4565434

Northamptonshire,
Staffordshire, Warwickshire,
Shropshire, Hereford and
Worcester, West Midlands

Nottingham Office
Anderson House, Clinton
Avenue, Nottingham
NG5 1AW.
Tel: 01159 693355

Derbyshire *(except High Peak District)*, Leicestershire,
Lincolnshire, Nottinghamshire

NORTH WEST REGION
Commercial Union House,
Alert Square, Manchester
M60 8AD
Tel: 0161 8338585

High Peak District of
Derbyshire, Cheshire,
Greater Manchester

Merseyside Office
Cressington House,
249 St. Mary's Road,
Garston, Liverpool L19 0NF.
Tel: 0151 427 8881

SCOTLAND
Franborough House,
123-157 Bothwell Street,
Glasgow G2 7JR.
Tel: 0141 204 2677

WALES
No. 3 Purbeck House,
Lambourne Crescent,
Llanishen Cardiff CF14 5GJ.
Tel: 01222 762636

**The Offices Of The Health And
Safety Executive**

HEAD OFFICES
Rose Court, 2 Southwark
Bridge, London SE1 9HF.
Tel: 020 7 717 6000

Magdalen House, Stanley
Precinct, Bootle, Merseyside
L20 3QZ.
Tel: 0151 951 4000

AREA OFFICES
South West
Inter City House, Mitchell
Lane, Bristol BS1 6AN.
Tel: 01179 886000

South
Priestley House, Priestley Road,
Basingstoke RG24 9NW.
Tel: 01256 404000

South East

3 East Grinstead House,
London Road, East Grinstead
RH19 1RR.
Tel: 01342 334200

London North
Maritime House,
1 Linton Road, Barking
IG11 8HF.
Tel: 020 8 594 5522

London South
1 Long Lane, London
SE1 4PG.
Tel: 020 7 5562100

East Anglia
39 Baddow Road,
Chelmsford CM2 0HL.
Tel: 01245 706200

Northern Home Counties
14 Cardiff Road, Luton
LU1 1PP.
Tel: 01582 444200

East Midlands
5th Floor, Belgrave House,
1 Greyfriars, Northampton
NN1 2BS.
Tel: 01604 738300

West Midlands
McLaren Building,
2 Masshouse Circus,
Queensway, Birmingham
B4 7NP.
Tel: 0121 6095200

Wales
Brunel House, Fitzalan Road,
Cardiff CF2 1SH.
Tel: 01222 263000

The Marches
The Marches House, Midway,
Newcastle-under-Lyme
ST5 1DT.

Tel: 01782 602300
North Midlands
Birkbeck House,
Trinity Square,
Nottingham NG1 4AU.
Tel: 01159 712800

South Yorkshire
Sovereign House,
110 Queen Street, Sheffield
S1 2ES.
Tel: 01142 912300

W & N Yorkshire
8 St. Pauls Street, Leeds
LS1 2LE
Tel: 01132 2834200

Greater Manchester
Quay House, Quay Street,
Manchester M3 3JB.
Tel: 0161 9528200

Merseyside
The Triad, Stanley Road,
Bootle, Merseyside L20 3PG.
Tel: 0151 4792200

North West
Victoria House, Ormskirk
Road, Preston PR1 1HH.
Tel: 01772 836200

North East
Arden House, Regent Centre,
Regent Farm Road,
Gosforth, Newcastle-upon-Tyne
NE3 3JN.
Tel: 0191 2026200

Scotland East
Belford House, 59 Belford
Road, Edinburgh EH4 3UE.
Tel: 0131 247 2000

Scotland West
375 West George Street,
Glasgow G2 4LW.

Tel: 0141 275 3000
The Data Protection Registrar
Wycliffe House, Water Lane,
Wilmslow SK9 5AF.
Tel: 01625 545700

**The Head Office Of The
Employment Tribunals**
Southgate Street,
Bury St. Edmunds
IP33 2AQ.
Tel: 01284 762171
Fax: (For Applications)
01284 706064

EQUAL OPPORTUNITES COMMISSION OFFICES

Wales
Windsor House,
Windsor Lane, Cardiff
CF1 1LB.
Tel: 01222 343552

Scotland
Stock Exchange House,
7 Nelson Mandela Place,
Glasgow G2 1QW.
Tel: 0141 248 5833

England
Oversees House, Quay Street,
Manchester M3 3HN.
Tel: 0161 833 9244

COMMISSION FOR RACIAL EQUALITY OFFICES

London (Head Office)
Elliot House,
10-12 Allington Street,
London SW1E 5EH.
Tel: 020 7 828 7022

Birmingham
Alpha Tower (11th Floor),
Suffolk Street, Queensway,
Birmingham B1 1TT.

Tel: 0121 7103000

Leeds
Yorkshire Bank Chambers
(1st Floor), Infirmary Street,
Leeds LS1 2JP.
Tel: 0113 3893600

Manchester
Maybrook House (5th Floor),
40 Blackfriars Street,
Manchester
M3 2EG.
Tel: 0161 8355500

Derby
31 Normanton Road,
Derby DE1 2GJ.
Tel: 01332 372428

Scotland
Hanover House, 45-51
Hanover Street, Edinburgh
EH2 2PJ.
Tel: 0131 226 5186

APPENDIX 1 – TIMECHART

A consolidated quick-guide to employment rights, their qualifying period and the time limit for complaint to an employment tribunal.

EMPLOYMENT RIGHT	QUALIFYING SERVICE	TIME LIMIT FOR COMPLAINT TO EMPLOYMENT TRIBUNAL
MATERNITY		
Right to 18 weeks maternity leave and return thereafter	None	3 months from the notified date of return and the employer's refusal to allow to return
Right to additional maternity leave of up to 29 weeks from the week of birth and return thereafter	1 year	3 months from the notified date of return and the employer's refusal to allow to return
Unfair dismissal due to pregnancy	None	3 months from the EDT
Written reasons for dismissal where the employee is pregnant or on maternity leave	None	3 months from the EDT
The right to statutory maternity pay Lower rate Higher rate	 26 weeks 26 weeks	3 months from the first day payment becomes due
Time off for ante-natal care	None	3 months from the date of the appointment refused by the employer

EMPLOYMENT RIGHT	QUALIFYING SERVICE	TIME LIMIT FOR COMPLAINT TO EMPLOYMENT TRIBUNAL
DISMISSAL		
Written reasons	1 year	3 months from the effective date of termination (EDT)
Unfair dismissal	1 year	3 months from the EDT
Unfair dismissal further to a business transfer	1 year	3 months from the EDT
Unfair dismissal connected with medical suspension	1 month	3 months from the EDT
Unfair dismissal where the employer has failed to offer re-engagement and the dismissal was connected with industrial action	1 year	6 months from the complainant's date of dismissal
Unfair dismissal for asserting a statutory right	None	3 months from the EDT
Unfair dismissal further to the exposure of a health and safety hazard	None	3 months from the EDT
Unfair dismissal related to national minimum wage	None	3 months from the EDT
Unfair dismissal for a reason connected with the Working Time Regulations	None	3 months from the EDT
Unfair dismissal of a shop worker for refusing to work on a Sunday	None	3 months from the EDT

EMPLOYMENT RIGHT	QUALIFYING SERVICE	TIME LIMIT FOR COMPLAINT TO EMPLOYMENT TRIBUNAL
REDUNDANCY		
Statutory Redundancy Pay	2 years	6 months from the EDT
Consultation with the recognised trade union	None	Complaint may be made before the dismissal or 3 months from the EDT
Time off to look for alternative employment	2 years	3 months from the first day time off should have been allowed

EMPLOYMENT RIGHT	QUALIFYING SERVICE	TIME LIMIT FOR COMPLAINT TO EMPLOYMENT TRIBUNAL
DISCRIMINATION		
Not to be discriminated against on the grounds of sex	None	3 months from the last act complained of
Not to be discriminated against on the grounds of race	None	3 months from the last act complained of
Equal pay	None	6 months from the EDT
Not to be discriminated against on the grounds of disability	None	3 months from the last act complained of

EMPLOYMENT RIGHT	QUALIFYING SERVICE	TIME LIMIT FOR COMPLAINT TO EMPLOYMENT TRIBUNAL
TRADE UNION MATTERS		
Time off to perform trade union activities	None	3 months from the date time off should have been given
Unfair dismissal for a reason connected with union membership or non-membership	None	3 months from the EDT
Exclusion or expulsion from a union	None	3 months from the last act complained of
Not to be justifiably disciplined by a union	None	6 months from the date of expulsion or exclusion
Compensation for being unjustifiably disciplined by a union	None	The claim must be made between 4 weeks and 6 months after the tribunal decision
To information and consultation with a recognised union further to a business transfer	N/A	3 months from the date of transfer
Where compensation is ordered in respect of the above but not paid for by the employer	N/A	3 months from the tribunal decision
To use the employer's premises for a union ballot	N/A	3 months from the employer's failure to allow the ballot
Not to be refused employment on the grounds of union membership	N/A	3 months from the act complained of

EMPLOYMENT RIGHT	QUALIFYING SERVICE	TIME LIMIT FOR COMPLAINT TO EMPLOYMENT TRIBUNAL
OTHER EMPLOYMENT RIGHTS		
Guarantee pay	1 month	3 months from the day pay is claimed
Statutory rights where the employer is insolvent	None	3 months from the Secretary of State's decision
Time off for public duties	None	3 months from the date of failure to allow time off
Written particulars of employment	1 month	3 months from the EDT
Itemised pay statement	None	3 months from the EDT
Pay on the grounds of medical suspension	1 month	3 months from the first day pay is claimed
Not to have unlawful deductions from pay	None	3 months from the last unlawful deduction
Contract claim by employee	None	3 months starting with the effective date of termination or the last day on which the employee worked

EMPLOYMENT RIGHT	QUALIFYING SERVICE	TIME LIMIT FOR COMPLAINT TO EMPLOYMENT TRIBUNAL
WORKING TIME REGULATIONS		
Right to daily rest	None	3 months from date when right should have been permitted
Right to weekly rest	None	3 months from date when right should have been permitted (or, if rest period extended over more than one day, date when right should have been permitted to begin)
Right to rest breaks	None	3 months from date when right should have been permitted
Right to compensatory rest in case where the above regulations are modified or excluded	None	3 months from date when right should have been permitted
Right to annual leave	13 weeks	3 months from date when right should have been permitted (or, if leave extended over more than one day, date when right should have been permitted to begin)
Right to payment in lieu of accrued holiday on termination of employment	None	3 months from date payment should have been made
Right to pay during annual leave	None	3 months from date payment should have been made

APPENDIX 2 – APPLICATION TO AN EMPLOYMENT TRIBUNAL – WRONGFUL DISMISSAL (BREACH OF CONTRACT).

EMPLOYMENT TRIBUNALS

Received at COIT	For office use
	Case Number Code Initials ROIT

Application to an Employment Tribunal

This form has to be photocopied. If possible, please use BLACK INK and CAPITAL letters
Where there are tick boxes, please tick the one that applies

1 Please give the type of complaint you want the tribunal to decide (for example: unfair dismissal, equal pay). A full list is given in booklet ITL1. If you have more than one complaint, please list all of them.

WRONGFUL DISMISSAL (BREACH OF CONTRACT)

2 Please give your details

Mr ☑ Mrs ☐ Miss ☐ Ms ☐

Surname *HADDOCK*
First Names *JOHN KEITH*
Date of Birth *12/7/56*
Address *150 MARNEY ROAD, SOUTH LONDON*

Post Code *SW1 4OU*
Telephone *020 7666999*
Daytime
Telephone *020 7666999*
(If we or ACAS need to contact you)

Please give an address to which we should send documents, if different from above.

AS ABOVE

Post Code

3 If a representive is acting for you, please give details.

Name *MR MURRAY FAIRCLOUGH*
Address *SURREY REPRESENTATION UNIT, SUTTON, SURREY*
Post Code *SM1 4DW*
Telephone *020 8662244*
Reference *MSCF*

4 Please give the dates of your employment

From *9th AUGUST 1999*

To *12th MARCH 2000*

5 Please give the name and address of the employer, other organisation or person against whom this compliant is being brought.

Name of employer, organisation or person.
MEGA INSURANCE SERVICES LTD
Address *HEAD OFFICE, 100 COMMERCIAL STREET, WEST LONDON*
Post Code *W1 3TP*

Telephone *020 7000111*

Please give the place where you worked or applied to work if different than above.

AS ABOVE

Address

AS ABOVE

Post Code

6 Please give what job you did for the employer (or what job you applied for). If this does not, please say what your connection was with the employer.

INSURANCE NEGOTIATOR

7 Please give the number of normal basic hours worked each week.

35 **Hours per week**

8 Please give your earning details.

Basic wage/salary

£ 15,000 : 00 p ANNUM

Average take home pay

£ 220 : 00 p WEEK

Other bonuses/benefits

£ 50 : 00 p MONTH

9 Unfair dismissal applicants only

Please indicate what you are seeking at this stage, if you win your case:

☐ **Reinstatement:** to carry on working in your old job as before. (An order for reinstatement normally includes an award of compensation for loss of earnings

☐ **Re-engagement:** to start another job or new contract with your old employer. (An order for re-engagement normally includes an award of compensation for loss of earnings

☐ **Compensation only:** to get an award of money

10 If your complaint is not about dismissal, please give the date when the action you are complaining about took place.

NOT APPLICABLE

11 Some types of case are heard by a Chairman alone unless a Chairman decides otherwise. All types of case can be heard by a Chairman alone if the parties agree. If you have any views on this matter indicate them here.

☐ *I would like my case to be heard by a Chairman alone.*

☑ *I would like my case to be heard by a Chairman and lay members.*

If you wish, give reasons for your preference.

NO REASON

12 Please give details of your complaint. If there is not enough space for your answer, please continue on a separate sheet and attach it to this form.

On Tuesday 12th March 1999 I was called into the office of my manager Mr Malcolm Blunt. He told me that my performance was wholly unsatisfactory and that accordingly he was terminating my contract of employment by giving me one weeks' notice, which would be paid in lieu of working. Mr Blunt handed to me a prepared cheque for the notice money along with my P45 and I was told to collect my belongings and leave the building, which I duly did. The disciplinary procedure in my contract of employment was not followed and my contract states I am entitled to one month's notice of termination (continued).

13 Please sign and date this form, then send it to the address given on page 2.

Signed Mr J.K.Haddock

Date 1st April 2000

APPENDIX 3 – APPLICATION TO AN EMPLOYMENT TRIBUNAL – UNFAIR DISMISSAL

EMPLOYMENT TRIBUNALS

Received at COIT	For office use
	Case Number Code Initials ROIT

Application to an Employment Tribunal

This form has to be photocopied. If possible, please use BLACK INK and CAPITAL letters
Where there are tick boxes, please tick the one that applies

1 Please give the type of complaint you want the tribunal to decide (for example: unfair dismissal, equal pay). A full list is given in booklet ITL1. If you have more than one complaint, please list all of them.

UNFAIR DISMISSAL

2 Please give your details

Mr ☐   Mrs ☑   Miss ☐   Ms ☐

Surname *GREGG–GILBEY*
First Names *EILEEN*
Date of Birth *18/4/64*
Address *THE COACH HOUSE, MAIN STREET, RYE EAST SUSSEX*
                    Post Code *TV31 6MT*
Telephone *01342 666999*
Daytime
Telephone *01342 666999*
(If we or ACAS need to contact you)

Please give an address to which we should send documents, if different from above.

AS ABOVE

                    Post Code

3 If a representive is acting for you, please give details.

Name *MR MURRAY FAIRCLOUGH*
Address *SURREY REPRESENTATION UNIT, SUTTON, SURREY*
                    Post Code *SM1 4DW*
Telephone *020 8662244*
Reference *MSCF*

4 Please give the dates of your employment

From *3rd FEBRUARY 1992*

To *12th MARCH 2000*

5 Please give the name and address of the employer, other organisation or person against whom this compliant is being brought.

Name of employer, organisation or person.
MEGA RETAILER LIMITED
Address *HEAD OFFICE, 99 MAIN STREET, RYE, EAST SUSSEX*
                    Post Code *TV31 5MT*

Telephone *01342 999666*

Please give the place where you worked or applied to work if different than above.

AS ABOVE

Address

AS ABOVE

                    Post Code

6 Please give what job you did for the employer (or what job you applied for). If this does not, please say what your connection was with the employer.

CLEANER AND SHELF–STACKER

7 Please give the number of normal basic hours worked each week.

40 **Hours per week**

8 Please give your earning details.

Basic wage/salary

£ *3,500* : *00* **p** *ANNUM*

Average take home pay

£ *55* : *00* **p** *WEEK*

Other bonuses/benefits

£ *5* : *00* **p** *MONTH*

9 **Unfair dismissal applicants only**

Please indicate what you are seeking at this stage, if you win your case:

☑ **Reinstatement:** to carry on working in your old job as before. (An order for reinstatement normally includes an award of compensation for loss of earnings

☐ **Re-engagement:** to start another job or new contract with your old employer. (An order for re-engagement normally includes an award of compensation for loss of earnings

☐ **Compensation only:** to get an award of money

10 If your complaint is not about dismissal, please give the date when the action you are complaining about took place.

NOT APPLICABLE

11 Some types of case are heard by a Chairman alone unless a Chairman decides otherwise. All types of case can be heard by a Chairman alone if the parties agree. If you have any views on this matter indicate them here.

☐ *I would like my case to be heard by a Chairman alone.*

☑ *I would like my case to be heard by a Chairman and lay members.*

If you wish, give reasons for your preference.

NO REASON

12 Please give details of your complaint. If there is not enough space for your answer, please continue on a separate sheet and attach it to this form.

On Tuesday 12th March 2000, my supervisor Mr Smith called me into his office. He said that I had mislabelled some produce and placed it on the wrong shelves in the store. I told him that I was not to blame for the mistake and that he should speak to my colleague Elizabeth Jones who could provide an explanation. Mr Smith sacked me without giving me the opportunity to defend my position. I believe I have been unfairly dismissed (continued).

13 Please sign and date this form, then send it to the address given on page 2.

Signed *Mrs E. Gregg-Gilbey*

Date *25th March 2000*